My Mother's GTO

Rick Sandine

Contents

396: Chevrolet's powerful engine that was dominant in the later 1960s

RAT MOTOR: a street nickname for Chevrolet's powerful 396 engine

SUPER COMMANDO 440: A powerful engine from Chrysler that dominated the streets in the late 1960s

MOPAR: Any car/engine/transmission or auto part made by Chrysler

MARKET/MARKET STREET: A long 10-mile commercial stretch of highway on the South side that was dotted by red lights and lightly patrolled by police at that time...

BELMONT: A busy, commercial highway on the North side that was dotted by red lights and lightly patrolled by police

ROUTE 304: A popular intersection - way out Belmont - where important street races would often occur

340: A blazingly fast small car, usually a Dodge Dart, that was feared on the street in the late '60s to early '70s

RAM AIR: A Pontiac engine option, introduced in the late 60s, that was an absolute killer in the 1/4 mile

TRI-POWER: A Pontiac powered by a high-compression 389, with 3, two-barrel carbs -giving the car dazzling acceleration

L-78: A powerful engine option- available on a Chevelle, Camaro, or Impala - with a solid lifter camshaft, and was rated at 375 HP.

Cast of Players

A 69 Judge GTO

A 66 Oldsmobile 442

A 67 GTO

A '62 Bonneville

A 65 Red Impala SS Convertable

A 65 Blue Catalina

A 65 GTO

A red 65 GTO

A 65 Impala SS

A 65 Corvette Stingray

A 64 GTO Convertible

A 66 396 Chevelle

A 67 GTO

A 68 SS Chevelle

A 67 Coronet RT

A 64 GTO

A 69 Superbee Dodge

A 68 Z28 Camaro

A 69 340 Dart Swinger

A 68 Charger RT

A 66 427 Corvette Convertible

A 1968 442 Convertible

A 1970 Buick GSX

A 1970 Buick GSX side view

A 1970 Ford Torino Cobra Jet

A gold 65 GTO

A 1981 Delorean Automobile

A 1970 SS 454 Chevelle

A 65 Catalina

A 69 Plymouth Roadrunner

A 68 SS Chevelle

A 69 GTO Convertible

A 69 Convertible

A 69 Plymouth GTX

A 68 GTO Convertible

A 70 Dodge Challenger

A 66 Oldsmobile 442

A 65 Bonneville

A 65 442

A 59 Plymouth Sport Fury

A 69 Dodge Dart Swinger 340

A 1970 Cutlass Rally

A 64 GTO

Chapter 1

SUMMER - 1952:

At the age of 4, I was a spoiled little brat. I always wanted Dad to take me **everywhere** he went: So I'd play **cry-baby**..."Dad, lemme go with you...I promise to behave."

Success! It worked!

On summer Saturday nights, Dad would take me to the stock car races at Canfield Speedway; about a 25-minute ride from Youngstown's north side - where we lived.

Dad and I always had a BLAST driving to the races: radio blaring - laughing; and singing along to all the 50s "hit parade" tunes.

Whenever we passed the **Chew Mail Pouch Tobacco** sign, the road ahead became wider and smoother...a long straightaway.

Then, I got an idea!... I decided I'd make a dare to Dad: "Dad, you think our car could go 100? It says **100** on the speedometer."

Dad - without hesitating - immediately **FLOORED** his 1949 V8 Mercury....

GR-RRRRRROOOOM!

Suddenly, it grew intense - watching the quivering speedometer needle...straining up to 90; then 95...and finally, 100!

Dad was cheering: "YAY...we did it!" I was jumping around the front seat like a crazed lunatic! We'd gone a hundred miles an hour...

WOW!

After that, on **every** outbound trip, we'd have the thrilling 'run up to 100.' Such fun! There was nothing else like it!

Occasionally, Dad's 49 Mercury would 'have a bad day'- faltering at 97 or 98; so that added an element of suspense.

Nevertheless, I was 'hooked' on SPEED - especially the **NOISE** from the powerhouse Mercury V8 – the "muscle car" of its day.

Growing up, it became even more extreme: Going fast! A loudly-roaring V8! It became my obsession! It was so much **FUN**! I couldn't get enough! I always wanted MORE.

Eventually, winter driving would corrode Dad's beloved 49 Mercury: And so, a sporty red 56 Ford Sunliner convertible - with a 312 Thunderbird V8 - now occupied our garage.

***

5 YEARS LATER

It was a Saturday, in late February of 1960. CBS was telecasting the 1960 Daytona 500 NASCAR race – as part of their 'Saturday CBS Sports Spectacular.'

Wow! I'd be able to watch the actual live telecast of the Daytona 500! How SPECTACULAR!

Plus, I'd be HOME ALONE:

Mom always got her hair done on Saturdays; and then would go shopping. Dad- a workaholic - always would be doing something job-related on Saturday.

The timing was perfect:

A week earlier, two brawny delivery men - struggling heavily – had installed a console Philco 32-inch TV - with two large stereo SPEAKERS - in our living room. It was PUMP up the VOLUME time!

When the race came on, I was in heaven! The thundering noise from all the stock cars was so LOUD, the "nik-naks" on Mom's coffee table were vibrating like Mexican jumping beans.

On the back straight away, I loved hearing the tremendously-loud **GR-RRRRR** noise - coming from all the cars running "flat-out."

But without realizing it - during the exciting, 3-hour race - I had gradually turned the volume ALL the WAY up.

Not real smart.

"BANG." I heard the garage door slam shut...Uh-oh.

Mom was home!

She came charging into the living room like an angry hornet - shouting hysterically..."**LOWER THAT! LOWER THAT, YOU CRAZY BOY! LOWER** that TV!"

Needless to say - growing older - I would NOT become her 'favorite son.' Not by a country mile.

By summer, 1962, our 56 Ford convertible had 'rusted out.' Its white top was turning grey.

Then, a SURPRISE: Mom and Dad came home driving a splendid, new, burgundy 1962 Pontiac Bonneville with an all-white interior.

A '62 Bonneville

Everyone looked stunned when they saw our new Bonneville. It was impossible NOT to notice this spectacular 2 door beauty! Lurking under the hood was the vaunted Pontiac 389 4-barrel (303 hp) engine; with power to spare. Mom- always with an eye for style - was the one who actually spotted it on the dealer's lot. Pinch me...was this a DREAM? A fast, beautiful Bonneville? The envy of all the neighbors? Yes!

Not much later - at a red light on Belmont Ave - a gold 62 Oldsmobile Starfire pulled alongside our car (right lane). I was riding shotgun: Dad had a surprise for me...the look on his face was the tip off. When the light changed, Dad and the Starfire were off!

VAR-R-R-OOOOOOOM....

A street race! **WOW**. Dad had the Bonneville floored... so incredibly **LOUD.** It was electrifying...shocking...mesmerizing: The Starfire- in the right lane - was staying DEAD even! The clamoring noise from two big V8 engines was almost deafening! I thought I was in heaven! During the harrowing race, I could plainly see the Olds driver's taut facial expression. He was actually clenching his teeth! He was out to WIN! But Dad acted cool and nonchalant - flashing me a big grin.

What an unbelievably close race! The big Bonny and the Starfire ended up in a tie. I couldn't believe it! It took me a while to catch my breath. What a life-changing experience!

I began thinking how much fun my life would be after turning 16: Then I'd get my DRIVER's LICENSE, and then head on over to Belmont! At 15, I could get an 'Ohio learner's permit' (i.e.) driving ONLY with a 'licensed adult.'

Ohio learner's permit? Blah...what fun was that? Who needs a chaperone? I wanted to drag-race on Belmont! Blast the radio! Burn some RUBBER.

Impress all the lovely ladies... honking the horn – driving by their houses. Let all the girls think this gorgeous Bonneville was MINE.

Yeah, man!

I began imagining all the places I'd be going to after getting my license.

It was April '64 when I passed my driver's test. Tears of joy! I could now drive the Bonneville ALONE! It seemed too good to be true!

And it was:

Dad put on the brakes with his **'restrictions'** (i.e.) no driving the car **ALONE**, until becoming more 'experienced.'

For me, a bitter conundrum. My urge to race on Belmont was 'put on hold.' Not to be denied, I kept thinking of tangible reasons for driving the big Bonneville.

Ah, yes! The LIBRARY!

I tried asking Dad; but he wasn't falling for it - turning a deaf ear when I pleaded... "I'll only be gone for an hour."

A few days later, Dad- looking a bit debilitated - sent me to Gray Drug Store, to buy Pepto Bismol.

Finally: My first time driving the Bonneville - ALONE. The next day, Mom came through BIGTIME - sending me to Aunt Mary's house - bringing her eggplant parmesan (Mom's specialty).

Aunt Mary - Mom's oldest sister - was absolutely delighted! She was so glad to see me....and the eggplant! YUMM!

After Aunt Mary devoured the eggplant, she forked over 5 dollars!

Then she held me "spellbound" for two hours- reminiscing about the good ol' days, when she was a first-grade school teacher in Youngstown's public school system.

It was a breakthrough. I was gone ALL afternoon - bringing the Bonneville home safe 'n sound.

The next day, Mom got a call from Aunt Mary; who enthusiastically spoke of me **as her FAVORITE nephew.**

This gave me an idea: To drive the Bonneville on a Friday night, I'd BROWNIE-UP Mom 'n Dad! Start by becoming the world's most helpful son - doing every home chore imaginable...*without* being asked.

How could it fail to win their approval? Mom was a clean freak. Dad was a neat freak. There were nearly enough cleaning agents around our house to open a Dollar store.

Now, I could imagine driving the Bonneville on *a Friday night* – wildly popular among my friends. No longer jealous of that wussy, Neil O'Malley; whose parents let him drive their car anytime he wanted.

I started with cutting the lawn. Clipping shrubs. Spreading peat moss. Planting geraniums. Weed-pulling. Cleaning cellar and garage. Climbing UP the ladder to do the window washing, etc.

To please Mom, I even cleaned out our dreaded kitchen junk drawer. Then I washed Dad's F-150 pickup...cleaning the cement dust from the interior.

He was shocked! It looked almost new!

That following Saturday, I helped Dad (a masonry contractor) move scaffold: a time-consuming, heavy-lifting job.

At the end of the tiring day, said Dad... *"Well Rick, you worked hard. So, tomorrow afternoon, you can have the car. But don't do anything silly - joyriding around with your friends."*

Joyriding around with my friends? **NO WAY!**

I had much *BIGGER* plans in mind:

After cleaning & polishing the BONNEVILLE into showroom condition, I would drive by Kathy Kowalski's house...hoping to see her on the front porch - listening to the radio and reading magazines.

Kathy lived on the other side of Belmont (not too far away); and man-o-man, what a knockout! She was totally UNIQUE: Drop-dead GORGEOUS: honey blonde hair, angelic blue eyes, perfect legs, perfect smile.... but NOT conceited.

At school, ALL the smokin' hot chicks had their noses stuck up high above the ozone layer; but NOT Kathy. She was friendly!

Every guy in school wanted to ask her out; but they were absolutely terrified about **being shot down.**

On a one- to- ten scale, Kathy was off the charts! She was Cinderella. Snow White. Goldie locks. Little Red Riding Hood - a fairy princess brought to life.

First week of my sophomore year, Kathy (a freshman) approached me as I was walking down the corridor. Suddenly, she winked 'n smiled at me - while walking in the opposite direction. **Wow!**

Sitting through Geometry class, I was rendered shell-shocked: Kathy **Kowalski ACTUALLY** had **winked at me!**

And why not? In my homeroom, Jenny Krumholtz thought I **was "cute."** But Jenny had reddish-purple acne; with a slightly crooked nose.

A definite **NO-GO.**

Sunday after 12 o'clock Mass; I went into serious car-cleaning mode - vacuuming the Bonney's interior...washing & waxing- polishing every square inch of chrome.

Even the INSIDE of the rear window, was wiped sparkling CLEAN. Lastly, I used Murphy Oil Soap to get the white interior looking new. After about 44 coats of Turtle wax, the car looked showroom new.

Dad saw it and exclaimed *"WOW."*

The entire ordeal had taken almost 4 hours. The Bonneville *even SMELLED* new. While taking a quick shower- in my mind's eye - I fantasized myself driving by Kathy's house: Blasting the radio - honking the horn and waving...pulling into her driveway.

Then, a surprised Kathy would go bounding jauntily down her porch steps - poking her head through the passenger window - saying..."*Wow Rick, your car looks new!*"

"Wanna go for a ride, Kathy, through *Mill Creek park?*" Of course, she would!

Driving through Mill Creek Park, I would effortlessly and casually **pop** the question:

"Hey Kathy....wanna go see Herman's Hermits at Stambaugh (auditorium) next Saturday night?"

Of course, she would! **WHY NOT?** Herman's Hermits were but a notch below the Beatles. Teenage girls sobbing, screaming...fainting, etc.

A date with Kathy Kowalski! The numero-uno hottie of the entire school! It would be blockbuster NEWS for sure!

Yeah man!

Crossing Belmont, it was all coming into focus, but turning onto her street, my heart sank like the Edmund Fitzgerald. I could clearly see her house: and no one was home. No car in the driveway. Front door shut. Porch deserted.

CURSES! I'd rolled snake eyes.

NOW WHAT?

Turning back onto Belmont, again my life was about to change: forever. Stopping at the next red light, I saw a glistening, navy blue 64 Impala SS - coming up beside me in the right lane.

Guy driving (mid-20s, crew-cut) glared at me disdainfully, as he pulled alongside...as if saying: *"Don't even try, punk."*

Instantly I felt this incredible, surging **ADRENALINE** rush - completely intimidated by this menacing-looking 327 SS Chevy.

I could FEEL my heart pounding in my chest:

lub-dub...lub-dub...lub-dub...lub-dub...lub-dub.

Unbelievable SUSPENSE...my FIRST EVER street race!

It was a two-minute red light; it felt like an eternity.

The light turned green! I came roaring away! - dead even with the SS Impala beside me.

VROOOOOOOOOM!

As he hit second gear, the loud CHIRP from his rear tires meant *BYE-BYE!*

I saw blue-gray smoke coming from his dual exhausts. I saw six big tail lights.

I was astonished! He was FIVE cars ahead; maybe more.

In street racer's parlance...he'd "blown my doors off"...decisively.

Instantly, I'd learned my lesson about the Chevy 327..."*THE LITTLE*

ENGINE THAT COULD."

The SS driver was undoubtedly gloating about the teen he'd just humiliated in Daddy's Pontiac - looking for me in his mirror.

However, I'd wisely turned down a side street. Who likes to be ridiculed after losing a drag race?

Defeat was humbling enough; but it was 100 times WORSE to have your opponent LAUGHING away - stopped beside him at the next light.

I kept reminding myself..."DON'T ever mess with a 327 Chevy again."

But racing the SS was electrifying. There's just no other way to describe all the emotions involved:

The chilling suspense waiting at the light. Pounding pulse. Sweaty armpits: hands gripped tightly to the steering wheel.

The screeching of tires. The acrid smell of blue tire smoke...the ROAR of two high-compression V8 engines! How could I ever FORGET that?

I decided to head home. But I wasn't too discouraged. The next Sunday afternoon, again Dad was letting me take the Bonneville for *a joy ride*.

But it was not to be a joyous occasion.

Turning onto nearby Fifth Avenue - a wide 4-lane street - I saw what appeared to be a silver-grey 64 LeMans - stopped ahead at the next red light.

'G-T-O' was emblazoned on this car's rear deck.

GTO? Hmmm...what's this? Something new? I'd never heard of any GTO.

The driver was an arrogant punk (early 20's) with a smart-azz expression on his face.

Even worse, he looked over at me- laughing like a hyena - greatly AMUSED about something.

"Smart azz. What's this jerk's problem? What's so funny?"

"I'll blow his stupid GTO right off the road!"

The light changed; I nailed the gas pedal to the floor!

And *LINGERING* alongside was the GTO!

Suddenly, he hit 2nd gear - then, like a streak of lightning - bolted away!

G-R-R-R-ROOOOOOOOOOOOOOOM!

WOW! The sight of the rapidly disappearing GTO left an indelible impression on me that NEVER would I forget!

It was unimaginable: what car on earth could have stayed with that lightning-quick GTO? God, was it ever FAST!

At the next red light ahead, I could imagine what this smart-alecky GTO driver was thinking: "What a stupid dolt...trying to race me in Daddy's Bonneville. Hey- where did he go?"

It was hide 'n seek time: I was parked nearby, hidden on a side street - not wanting to be ridiculed by this brazen punk in his hellfire GTO.

Nevertheless, I remained in total SHOCK! The GTO had whipped the Bonneville by an entire BLOCK!

What was I thinking? Why didn't I know? There was no POSSIBLE way to beat a GTO.

Chapter 2

A '64 GTO

JUNE- 1964:

HORRORS!

After getting **demolished** by a ferocious 64 GTO, it was time to stop being so **incredibly** STUPID - **thinking** to myself..."Look Bozo - **GET REAL: Dad's** Bonneville might **seem** fast, but it **ain't** gonna beat no nasty-azz GTO."

Now, I realized I had to be **super careful** about WHO and WHEN to race. **Ergo,** race **ONLY** cars that were **"BONNEVILLE-sized!" Yeah - start using some common sense.**

But the **siren song** of **an ADRENALINE RUSH** - surging throughout **my** body (and mind) - **had become a COMPULSION...an obsession! There was nothing else like it!**

Street racing was ACTION. High SUSPENSE. Staring down the other driver. Trying to psyche him out. Or not letting him psyche you. Trying to control ones nerves JUST BEFORE the light was about to turn green. Then, VROOOM - off to the races! Pure excitement! It could occur at the NEXT red light.

So, after running an errand for Mom or Dad, **I'd gleefully scoot up to Belmont - seeking my next "buzz" behind the wheel.**

But drag racing in DAYTIME on a busy thoroughfare (Belmont) was downright PERILOUS; and of course, **really** STUPID.

It was around noon: I was lined up **next to** a 64 Buick Wildcat...light changes, and we both went storming away. **V-RRROOM**!

Then, **WATCH OUT! A swaying,** lumbering **Stroh's** beer truck pulled haphazardly onto Belmont - **right** in front of us!

PANIC STOP...I jammed on the power brakes! SCREEEECH!

My God! I'd come within 5 feet of SMASHING-UP the Bonneville! Unbelievable STUPIDITY! It would have been a calamity!

Nevertheless, it was a lesson learned: "Thou SHALT NOT drag race in DAYTIME."

One night, not much later, Dad and I were on the porch listening to the Indians. They had just defeated the odious New York Yankees.

Dad **(a die-hard Cleveland fan)** was rapturous with **joy.**

Judging the time right**,** I asked**...**"Hey Dad, can I run up to McDonalds with the car**?"**

"Okay; but be careful. And be back home in an hour**."**

Immediately, I drove up the block to pick up Frankie Malone; another hard-core street racing addict. Frank- riding shotgun - always acted as my official "co-pilot."

In a bolt of inspiration, Frank made a suggestion I could NOT REFUSE**...**"Hey, **let's** drive by Loretta **Berman's** house."

What a fantastic IDEA!

I was thinking**...**"Wait till **Loretta** sees me driving this gorgeous car."

And who was Loretta Berman? **Undoubtedly**, the most sultry-looking maiden in the entire neighborhood....**5' 7'**... slender curvy legs... and what a BODY!

In fact, that **cool** 70s **hit** song, **"She's** a Brick **House"** (Commodores) may have been written about her.

Often, Loretta would parade around the neighborhood in her **short shorts**- practically **s**topping traffic.

She was usually on her front porch in the summertime.

Turning the corner, we were both dying with anticipation...Loretta lived only a minute away.

She was indeed on the front porch - sitting with one of her BOYFRIENDS.

CURSES!

We "reacted" by slowly driving **past her house** - yelling..."Hey Loretta**!**" Then I **went zooming** up the block full speed...honking the horn like some lunatic moron.

After a quick spin up **and down** Belmont, we decided to drive by her house again.

Maybe the pesky boyfriend had departed.

Nope. There he was.

Now what?

Time for an **"encore"** performance.

Again - driving by slowly - we both yelled... "hey Loretta" and then ZOOM, I went up her street again - full throttle**! - desperate** to be noticed by lovely Loretta**! (I wanted to be SURE she saw me driving the big Bonny)**

Time to head home. It was well past one hour.

Uh-oh... Dad **was waiting for me outside** on the driveway - all bent outta shape..."You irresponsible, **stupid,** reckless *!!#@**%#*****#*##*!"

"What's wrong, Dad?"

"Mrs. Schroeder JUST called, and told us...'**You** know your son keeps driving up my street, GOING 90 MILES an hour!"

Mrs. Schroeder and my parents would often **"chat"** after Sunday Mass. She lived five houses up from Loretta Berman.

Dad was ranting and **RAVING…**"You imbecile**! No** more taking out the car alone; unless **it's** an emergency**!"**

Total disaster! Now **I'd** be the one sitting on the porch at night.

Dad **angrily** began calling me a "simpleton" - completely jerked-off about my reckless **driving…**"You **could've** run over and killed somebody**! My car insurance would get canceled!"**…etc.

Mom offered her support - telling Dad: "Joe. **Don't EVER** let that crazy boy drive at night**!"**

Frankie **wasn't** yet 16 (no **driver's** license). So**, we'd** WALK a mile up to Belmont, to the "RED **BARN"**- the **new** hangout.

Almost overnight, **McDonald's** had become practically deserted.

Red Barn was a BLAST; with its huge parking lot. The IDEAL place for burning rubber; laying "strips"**-** driving the rent-a-cop completely delirious.

"BURN BABY BURN**."**

RED BARN was **JAMMIN.'** Everyone sitting in cars. Radios blaring. Horns honking. People congregating. Cars with raised hoods: **some** were tri-power GTOs.

Red **Barn's** "carnival-like" atmosphere was where all the baddest-fastest cars would go…**the PLACE to be SEEN! Action central!**

Nightly, **there'd** be an endless parade **of** cars - laying strips. Honking horns. Radios **blasting.** Yelling. **Laughter.** Taunting **and**

jeering between 2 drivers: "Hey man...wanna **race** that **thing** for 5 bucks**?"**

One night**,** early in July - some arrogant punk, Chipper Armando, comes cruising through Red Barn in his red, 327 fuel-injected 64 Corvette - acting like **he's** the greatest thing since color television.

Not a minute later **it** was Jerry LaGuardia **pulling** in**, with** his awesome 63 Impala dual-quad 409. Time for the big showdown!

Immediately, the big race was on! Everyone wanted to see it. The plan was set. **Race way out on Belmont Ave extension..."out in the sticks." No cops to worry about.**

"Gentlemen...start your engines."

Like forming a funeral procession, cars were exiting the **parking lot, one-by- one - following** the 2 "contenders**." At** least 20 cars; maybe more.

We were 4 guys riding in Danny **Miller's 55** Chevy. Frank & I were in the back seat. Then, it got a little "HAIRY**."**

Going up Belmont, a white 62 Ford Galaxie - 3 females in front - pulls alongside us in the right lane.

Then, **on spur of the moment**, Jerry Landis- riding shotgun - drops his bermudas **- sticks his butt out the window** - and MOONS the ladies to our right!

"YEEK**!**" They went hysterical**:**

Blonde girl driving (about 19) jams on the brakes - almost causing a "chain reaction" collision with everyone behind.

It was mayhem! I could hear the **girls'** frantic screams coming from the Ford**!** And who could blame them? I almost screamed. A **terrible** sight **I'd** never seen before:

Landis was horrifically "butt-ugly." His **butt** was **actually "furry"** - like some wild African orangutan. Or like the "Wolfman" in those old scary movies; with his fuzzy rear end.

AAAARGH! **I nearly flipped-out! A hairy butt? Ugh. I COULD NOT believe what I was seeing!** God, was it ever a GHASTLY sight

- looking as if **he'd** applied "growth **hormone**" to his butt to thicken the **furry** hair. **YECK.**

Never saw anything like it! (I still remember it) **Riding way out Belmont, I was in still in mild shock for awhile.**

Not surprisingly, **lunatic** Jerry Landis became known as "Moon." The name stuck for a long time thereafter. **A real-life wild man.**

Another disaster: after traveling way out Belmont, just before the race started; a cloudburst of rain **came cascading down.** Reluctantly - windshield wipers clicking - the entire parade turned around and headed for home.

It was now past one **o'clock** in the morning.

After "tip-toeing" into the house, I fell soundly asleep.

Next thing I knew, there stood Dad beside my bed. It was 7 AM.

"**Go** out in the garage and put on your WORK shoes...**we're** on ten-inch today."

Terrible news to awaken to! I would be carrying HEAVY 10-inch cement blocks all day - swinging them up on the scaffold- to be laid by a crew of 10 bricklayers.

This was HARD work - like a prison chain gang. **You'd** sweat! And NO sitting down.

But Dad "paid well." His men all loved him. Plus, we had a RADIO.

Again, my life would change:

"Coffee **break**"...it was 9:30 AM:

I would be the **gopher -** go for the **men's** coffee **'n** donuts**.**

Just then, a huge cement block delivery truck pulled in - blocking in **Dad's** F-150 pick-up.

Scratch one coffee break.

"Here Ricky, take my car...and remember, I ONLY drink tea**.**"

It was Winfield Davis - master scaffold builder - who also ran the cement mixer.

He handed me his keys.

Coffee break saved!

Parked roadside, was his blue 2-door 1959 Plymouth SPORT FURY; with its **ornate** front grille; and dual exhausts. **Winfield's** car was so HUGE; and so COOL - especially for a "work car**.**"

A '59 Plymouth Sport Fury

Inside, beneath all the cement dust, was **a** chrome-plated dashboard; **much** like my uncle **Arthur's** Cadillac Eldorado. **Having never driven a "Mopar" (Chrysler product) the interior looked so "foreign" to me. You put the key in the ignition "upside down."** Instead of a steering column shift, there were four huge chrome buttons **on the dashboard...Chrysler'** infamous "push-button" torque flight transmission.

The **gargantuan** back seat looked like it could sleep a "family of four." What a monster-**sized** car! **No house trailer needed.**

Turned on the radio: "Little GTO" (Ronnie 'n the Daytonas) was **risin'** up the **Top-40** charts.

I now was "cleared for takeoff**."**

Starting it up: VA-RROOOOOM!

Wow...**Winfield's** Plymouth sounded like **it was rarin'** to GO! Both hands on the wheel**! I had no idea what to expect from this "foreign" car. It was so different!**

Then, after just "touching" the gas- the front end jumped up - like a wild horse. **WHOA...I knew I was in for one helluva ride:**

But I had no idea such a huge car **could** be so unbelievably FAST!

Pulling onto the road, I put the hammer **DOWN....VARRROOOOOOOM.**

Wow...my HEAD SNAPPED back so violently, It was like riding the "Wildcat" - Youngstown's fearsome fabled wooden roller coaster, at Idora Park. This car accelerated with such velocity, it practically knocked me into the BACK seat! I was laughing!

Then, I realized that this unbelievable sensation of forward motion was due to the incredibly-quick shifting, 3-speed torqueflite transmission. It shifted speeds so quickly (1-2-3) there were no discernable pauses between shifts. It was just straight ahead, pure acceleration! Winfield's Plymouth literally flew down the road - like a wild banshee.

On the return trip, after pulling out onto the highway, I decided to floor it again...VAR-OOoooooom. Winfield's car seemed so fast, it was almost like a blur, the way the lines on

the road were going by! This car screamed! Even to today, it remains one of the fastest cars I ever drove!

What a FUN car!

Winfield's car had the optional Mopar 394 cubic-inch V8: with a Carter AFB four-barrel carburetor. 10.5 to one compression. High-lift hydraulic camshaft. Forged rods. Dual-breaker distributor. Probably cranking out close to 400 hp.

A GENUINE street beast! And such a blast to drive!

Back on the job, I handed Winfield his keys:

"Hey Win...did you know that your car has a high-performance, high-compression 394?" Winfield smiled wide; but he was totally clueless about what I was talking about.

All the rest of that day, I got more and more "resentful" toward Dad's Bonneville.

Problem was, I'd "tasted blood"...you know how that goes:

Once one experiences the tumultuous joy of driving a super fast car; never again can one be satisfied - or even tolerate - driving a SLOWER car. It's our human nature.

And besides - driving Dad's big, two-ton Bonneville - I was losing badly on the street - to the point where I EXPECTED to get blown away!

Even worse: this loser mentality meant no more suspense at red lights: And of course, no more adrenaline rush - taking away the fun and drama of racing on the street.

Damn...why couldn't the Bonneville be quicker? Compared to Winfield's Sport Fury, it was a like driving a lumbering, hulking concrete truck! Pitiful.

Ah**....**the obvious **solution: A goat! Like** the lyrics **from** the big hit song, **"Little GTO"...**"I would **save** all my money**....AND BUY A** GTO**."**

But with my **zero-sum** bank account, I had a long way to **go**.

Chapter 3

SUMMER 1964:

The GTO craze was sweeping over America! Pontiac's tire-frying GTO was just what every American loved:

Getting somewhere in a HURRY!

Ronnie & the Daytona's hit record, "Little GTO," climbed to #4 on the USA "top-40" hit charts.

People were fascinated with a car that could do zero to sixty in less than 5 seconds. You'd be an instant celebrity if you were wheeling around town in a 64 GTO!

Everyone wanted Pontiac's amazing GTO - especially ME. But in reality, having some "disposable income" (i.e.) cash on the barrel head...or in the local bank; was the only way I'd ever be driving any GTO.

Always the foolish squanderor – I hadn't managed to save any of my paper route profits since I was 13. Not real smart.

Saving for a rainy day? No way. A scrooge I was not. My current net worth approached sub-zero (i.e.) dire straits.

Sadly, I could only wish for a GTO - the most electrifying, astonishing car to EVER hit a showroom.

But I was totally obsessed: nothing else mattered. That entire summer, all I could think about was driving - or riding in a GTO!

After Labor Day, it was back to high school - my junior year. Finally, my life took a turn for the better. MUCH better.

As fate may have it, seated (alphabetically) in front of me was Dwight Patterson: a "natural-born" lady killer - with a wise-cracking, "jocular" personality to match.

We had a blast during class and became great friends.

"Bad-boy" Dwight - always passing notes - often would provoke me into boisterous laughter, right in the middle of class.

If he had been born in earlier times, Dwight may have "gone Hollywood" - perhaps becoming the next Clark Gable, or Errol Flynn. A really handsome devil he was indeed!

He had girls galore - following him down the corridors. The only thing missing were the sunglasses and autograph pad.

Dwight was Mr. Cool... the best-dressed guy in SCHOOL, with that certain "aura" around him. And like Tom Cruise, Dwight had "ALL the right moves" - so every girl "wanted his bod."

Whenever Dwight walked down the hall, girls became "groupies" - practically melting at his feet. Soon, the groupies began using me as a "clearing house" of information, i.e., "Why doesn't Dwight pay attention to me?" Or, "Why did Dwight stand me up Friday night?"... "Why doesn't Dwight ever call me?" etc.

Occasionally, I'd ask Dwight about his "Svengali-like" ability to hold lovely ladies spellbound. Always, he'd reply... "Ya gotta treat 'em like shet!"

What? No way! Treating a hot lady like sh*t? Impossible. Improbable. It was a lesson I NEVER would learn. Whenever using my archaic, "nicey-nice" approach, chicks would ROLL their eyes - then have me heading back to the "dugout" - after striking out. The LAST thing pretty ladies want is some sweet-talking jerk -

giving compliments; so boring! Even better, Dwight - like me - was a GTO fanatic! His family had assets, with his father running a trucking company and his Mom, a math teacher.

Relentlessly, Dwight would 'lobby' his pappy to buy him a GTO:

Said Dwight... "My father knows some used car guy with a red tri-power on his lot. It's looking really good!"

Wow, a TRI-POWER GTO! I began imagining going through Red Barn - riding shotgun. The focus of everyone's attention (i.e.) girls. Of course, my dream would go unfulfilled. There would never be any tri-power GTO.

After making inquiries about car insurance, Dwight's father bought him a new 65 Impala SS convertible. And what a car! 327 4-speed. Cherry red. White interior. White convertible top. It was stunningly beautiful and hauled azz!

A 65 Impala SS convertible

As it turned out, whenever Dwight promised to pick me up on a Friday night...always, I'd always be "stood up." (i.e.) left at the doorstep.

Dwight would instead head for 'greener' pastures. It became a routine. He was a determined "home run hitter." None of this "first, second, or third base" stuff: Dwight went for it all.

One Friday night in mid-October, he actually did show up at my house: I was surprised to no end - seeing Dwight's red SS Impala in my driveway.

I thought we'd be going to our high school dance; there would be ladies galore! Plus, I always practiced my dancing in our basement, especially to this one Motown song by Marvin Gay.

But no high school dance on this night:

"Diabolical" Dwight had other plans in mind: He'd pay a home "visit" to see Susie Shanlon, a slinky-looking dishwater blonde - determined to hit his next "home run."

Pulling into her driveway (mom n' dad out for the evening), Dwight literally sprang from the car like a hungry leopard - telling me... "Wait here; I'll be out in fifteen minutes." (i.e.) Two's company...three's a crowd.

He left the keys in the ignition so I could listen to the radio.

Waiting alone in the dark lonely driveway, I felt like a gullible, idiotic moron - sitting in the driver's seat: playing with the console 4-speed shifter...blasting the radio (what fun).

A half-hour passed. Then 45 minutes... one hour. Evidently, Dwight and Slinky Sue weren't playing "spin the bottle." Finally, after 90 minutes, Dwight emerged from the side door - looking immensely proud - reeking of perspiration... saying little. (Obviously, he'd hit a LATE-INNING, grand-slam home run.)

Two weeks later, the Friday night junior class party was to be held at Pioneer Pavilion in Mill Creek Park. Sure to be there were Jeanie Hoffman and best friend Barbie McNeil. Two slick chicks with bodies to match.

Plan was that Dwight and I would make the grand appearance after 11. Effortlessly, he'd talk these two hotties into a ride home, with yours truly in the back seat, with Barb McNeil and her curvy legs.YES. We were planning it like two bank robbers before a heist: Dwight would pick me up at 9 pm. We'd cruise around town in the Impala; and finally, head out to the class party at EXACTLY 11 pm - just like Starsky 'n Hutch! (teamwork). It was the night of the party - Friday, around 8:30 pm. I was all "decked out" with my new penny loafers, pleated beige slacks, and my new button-down "madras" shirt. Man, was ever prepared to rock that party!

Nevertheless, "diabolical" Dwight would be up to his "old tricks."

Ominously, 9 o'clock had passed...and where was Dwight?

Then 9:30.

Then 9:45

Panic time...WHERE in the world was Dwight Patterson? DAMMIT!

Finally, around 10, I called his house. His mother answered: "Why Dwight left the house almost two hours ago." Obviously, Slinky Susie had "distracted" horny Dwight again.

NOW WHAT?

Time to execute "plan B."

Having performed numerous house chores every day, my parents had "warmed up" about permitting me to drive the Bonneville on a Friday night. I decided to go for broke - heading to the living room.

Dad was reading his newspaper:

"Hey, Dad, Dwight didn't show up to take me to the party. Could I please have the car? I'll be super careful and be home before midnight."

"Ask your mother."

Mom was lying in bed - watching TV.

"Hey, Mom...Dad says I can have the car. Is it OK with you?"

Apparently not.

Springing from her bed in a fit of fury, she ran to the living room, screeching hysterically: "Joe...JOSEPH! Don't you DARE let him have the car! We'll lose our house!"

I was stunned. Initially, I could not see the correlation. How would my taking the Bonneville out could cause the loss of our family home? How so? It made no sense.

Sulking in my bedroom, finally, it dawned upon me: My propensity to drive fast would surely cause a calamitous collision - perhaps death/serious bodily injury to passengers in the other car. An aggressive personal injury lawyer would sue for six figures. My parents' hard-earned home – would be auctioned off to pay said damages.

"Kill all the lawyers!" (every last one)

The situation had become hopeless: A high-powered V8 car in my hands was just too much anxiety for my parents to bear.

As the school year flew by, NEVER again would I be able to take out the Bonneville on Friday nights. Dad was always fighting me with his pathetically lame argument - saying... "Too many drunks out driving on Friday nights." (i.e.) You'll stay home and watch "Twilight Zone."

During all this time, "Hollywood Dwight" had fallen victim to "Elvis Presley Syndrome."

Yes, indeed, the iconic Elvis Presley. SUPER STAR entertainer. Could've had his pick of ANY female in the world, then ends up choosing that (ugh) mascara-laden, taciturn, plain-jane Priscilla - proving that, indeed, love REALLY is blind.

Dwight had done likewise: Could've had his pick- ANY lady he desired! They all lined up before him. And you guessed it! Final pick? - that slinky, skinny-minnie (no booty) Susie Shanlon. (tsk tsk).

Evidently, a little intimacy goes a long way.

Time flies: Summer 1965 was "just around the corner,"- ushering in the sensational, new, even FASTER 65 GTO!

Pontiac engineers had vastly improved its legendary 389 cubic inch motor - a stroke of mechanical genius. Featured were state-of-the-art, quick-bleed hydraulic valve lifters. High-lift McKellar camshaft. 421 Super-Duty heads. D-shaped engine ports. Transistorized ignition. Performance suspension.

The all-new 65 GTO literally exploded with tire-scorching, neck-snapping excitement! First time I saw a 65 GTO... Wow...was it ever STUNNING! A real jaw-dropper!

The 65 GTO literally defined the word "WOW."

The gorgeous look of the car...Wow.

The astonishing acceleration...Wow.

People would see it- going down the street - and say, "WOW."

The all-new 65 GTO could go-go-go!

Seems that Pontiac had tried to come up with the *perfect car*...and SUCCEEDED.

Wow...*perfection*! No way to top that!

Chapter 4

A gorgeous gold '65 GTO

SPRING: 1965

Johnnie Marino - one of my most memorable characters - sat across the aisle from me in 4th period History. Since Johnnie hated to study, and the teacher hated him, I'd let

Johnnie "scope" off my test paper (i.e.) cheat. Otherwise, he would've gotten an "F."

It was a PERFECT arrangement because Johnnie would be obligated to ME!

Since he drove a new tiger gold 65 GTO, I figured it would be my absolute best shot at (finally) riding in a 65 GTO! I couldn't WAIT! My fantasy, about to become REALITY!

Johnie Marino's family had "class." They were "loaded" – owning a thriving grocery store. They resided in the affluent section of Liberty township - living in a magnificent 2 story brick house; with perfect taste in furnishings (puttin' on the ritz)

In their garage, was Johnny's shiny new, tiger gold GTO.

And in their basement was a posh, Brunswick, SLATE pool table; with web pockets; and a beautiful, plush gold cloth cover. The very best pool table money could buy- truly fit for a KING! Nice.

First time Frank and I played on it - we flipped out. Wow, from what we were used to, it was like we'd gone to "billiard heaven." Remarkably, Johnnie's table even SMELLED expensive - unlike the repulsive, stained, torn-cloth tables at dismal "Northside Lanes," where Frank and I would go on weekends to bowl and shoot pool. When you opened the entrance door at North side lanes, you were hit with a sort of a peculiar, "funny" smell. Sure, all bowling establishments had that familiar "bowling alley" smell. But at crappy North Side Lanes, when you opened the entrance door, it was like walking into some sweaty men's locker room - smelling like old tennis shoes.

Since the place lacked ventilation, a gas mask was highly recommended before entering the Men's room. Their decrepit, rental bowling shoes looked as if they'd been manufactured during the Spanish-American War Era (circa: 1898)

Hunger could present a problem: Their hot dogs were COLD.

Even worse: If one wanted a cheeseburger...WOE to THEE! It was either pay up or shut up. I even considered packing a brown-bag lunch (egg salad sandwich).

WORST of all was the owner's "pimply" 19 year old son: He was the "manager," poised arrogantly behind the cash register - acting like he was king shet.

When paying, I hated to even look him in the face. Zit-man. Pizza-face. Crater face. Those were the "preferred terms" in the 60s for one who had a terminal case (acne): i.e. the "Critical Face Theory."

Since there was no other competition on the North side, the cheapskate owner - a world-class skinflint - knew he held a captive audience; so he knew he could "get away with it." (i.e.) spending zero money to fix it up.

But no more.

What a pleasure to go to Johnny Marino's opulent house on weekends. Frank and I were our glory - shooting pool on Johnny's extravagant table.

Johnny Marino - being a spoiled, only child - always had to be the center of attention. One could best describe him as "quirky"...unpredictable: somewhat of a dichotomy (i.e.) a Jeckle 'n Hyde personality.

In other words, sometimes he'd be a JERK, and sometimes not.

He had a wise-cracking, self-assured exterior. But on the other hand, Johnny could be a really good guy - fun to be around.

That May (1965) I first rode in Johnny's tiger gold 65 GTO....4-barrel (335 hp) with black interior; with a two-speed automatic console shift.

Johnny's growling- howling GTO was lightning-quick on the street!

Such incredible TORQUE! Upon full acceleration - my body was pressed back VIOLENTLY into the bucket seat! I felt like an astronaut undergoing G-force training. It was unbelievable. Addicting. Astonishing. Exciting!

Yes, I'm going way overboard here; but that's the effect of a GTO, the first time I ever rode in one. It actually transformed my life.

From that minute on, I made a vow: someday soon, I'd have my own 65 GTO (a dream unfulfilled).

However, wild man Johnnie would beat his new GTO like an old, dusty doormat. I thought he'd gone completely loco - "DWI"- driving while insane (a felony)

Lunatic Johnnie would floor the gas while moving the transmission selector between "LO" and "DRIVE" - the car jerking up & down like a Brahma bull at a rodeo. Total insanity!

Indeed, that was one unfortunate goat.

Johnnie loved performing his rodeo "act" - usually at night. His GTO bouncing up and down Belmont. Then, he'd drive "triumphantly" through the Red Barn parking lot - seeking "center stage."

And what better 'stage' than the Red Barn?- which, by 1965, had "evolved" into 3 clearly-defined "social classes."

Lowest class were the GREASERS - wearing their "traditional" greaser uniform: sweaty, grimy, yellowish white T-shirt...short sleeves rolled up to the arm pits. Pack of Camels (cigarettes) in the shirt pocket. Hair oiled "stylishly" with Brylcreem.

Being "neglectful" of their personal hygiene, you could smell them from five feet away. Greasy finger nails were "de rigueur."

Not surprisingly, no one wanted go near them - especially girls.

Then there was the next class... the "REGULARS" - those who drove "nondescript" cars - serving as the "audience" for the top class; the CELEBRITIES (i.e.) those who drove the muscle cars.

Drive into the parking lot in a hot MUSCLE car? - instantly, you were a Red Barn celebrity! And guess who quickly became Red Barn's most foremost celebrity?

Nightly, Johnnie would recklessly drive around the parking lot...horn honking...burning rubber...radio booming...arguing with the rent-a-cop - daring ANYONE to race him on Belmont.

Police on Belmont? No way! The Liberty cops were too busy guarding Plaza donuts. Traffic tickets were an afterthought.

Back then, Liberty township had full coffers of tax money, from the many affluent people who resided there.

In the 60s, police were not "revenuers" like today's arrogant cops. Speed traps have NOTHING to do with safety. Americans have been brainwashed that "speed kills." Not so:

Sure, "speed kills"- but ONLY IF you collide with someone (or something).

Statistically, 90% of all USA traffic fatalities occur at RED LIGHT intersections; it's here where "an in irresistible force often meets an immovable object" (i.e.) Physics 101.

But it's not just those "red light runners" who cause the mayhem.

It's those YELLOW LIGHT RUNNERS! They're the ones to be aware of!

Picture this:

An impatient, hurried driver- coming from the intersecting street - interprets a yellow traffic signal as a sign to SPEED UP, and "KA-BOOOM"- he "T- bones" a hapless car in the middle of the crossway.

"ATTENTION...clean-up at Elm and Maple."

So buckle up... and ALWAYS be on the lookout at **ANY** red light. It was late June, about 10 PM. Colin Blakely- who's daddy was an MD - showed up at Red Barn- driving a glistening new, tuxedo-black 65 Oldsmobile 442; with RED interior...a really intimidating color combination.

Not surprisingly, It caused quite a stir. Blakley's 442 was gorgeous and SUPER fast!

Immediately, calls arose: Johnnie's GTO vs. Blakley's 442. Champ vs Challenger. Johnny didn't worry: So far, nobody had "whupped" his goat.

The race was set: late Saturday night, way out Belmont, past Route 304, where no cops ever roamed.

Bets were placed. Johnnie was heavily favored. The 65 GTO's reputation was bulletproof. Tri-power GTOs were Red Barn's "sacred cows."

That year, 442s were the "new cars on the block" – having something to "prove." But they were more than well equipped to rise up to the task: stiff competition for ANY GTO.

The 442 had a 400 cubic inch engine. A close-ratio 4-speed trans; with ultra-efficient, flow-thru Walker dual exhaust pipes. With a good stick-shift driver, the 442 emerged as a street machine NEVER to be taken lightly.

Nevertheless, the "coup de gras" of the 65 GTO was its extraordinary, high compression 389 cubic inch engine.

It was about 1AM - the night of the highly-anticipated race: Red Barn's parking lot was mobbed- the pre-race "buzz" was overwhelming.

At least 30 cars followed the two way out Belmont extension to watch the big match-up. Blakely's 442 and Johnny's GTO were like two heavyweight boxers - waiting in their corners for the slugfest to commence:

Then, it began to "spit" rain: (i.e.) not enough to put on the wipers; but just enough to slightly wet the windshield.

The two lined up: but with a "moist" track - upon "GO" - both cars went fishtailing and wheel-hopping sideways. Ergo; race postponed on account of rain.

Too bad. Never again would these 2 "Titans" of the Red Barn ever line up to race one-another.

One month later - first Sunday after school had resumed - I was sitting on my porch.

Surprise! Johnnie in his beautiful gold GTO pulled into the driveway:

"Hey Sandy, wanna go for a ride up Belmont?"

Riding shotgun, instantly, I sensed his GTO as being SLOWER.

After a summer of protracted abuse, the trans had loosened up. The cylinders were burned (loss of compression) - the universal joint creaking. After turning onto Belmont, up ahead, we saw a gleaming, burgundy 65 Impala SS at the next red light (right lane).

This 65 Impala looked showroom new. It was stunningly beautiful. Absolutely gorgeous.

But something was peculiar about this SS Impala: Rather than 327 fender badges, were these large, multi-colored crossed flag emblems: "396 Turbo-Jet."

The SS driver (mid-20s, clean cut) was coy - "pretending" not to notice us beside him.

On his radio I could distinctly hear "LIAR-LIAR" (pants on fire) by the Castaways. Just then, he turned down the volume...a sure sign he'd race.

Suddenly, the light turned green: It was UNREAL.

RH-E-E-E-E-E-E-O-WOOOM! Both cars were accelerating in a clamor of screeching, thundering noise!

The SS Impala began fishtailing sideways toward the curb - surrounded by a large, swirling cloud of grey-blue tire smoke! Wow...was it ever loud! The driver seemed a bit uncertain. We were about a car length ahead.

Astoundingly, after the SS driver hit 2nd gear, he caught up to us; then hitting 3rd, he began "easing away."

We were stunned! By the time he hit 4th, this nasty SS was ahead by about 3 and a half cars! Johnny's GTO had suffered a crushing, embarrassing defeat! SHOCKING indeed!

Pulling alongside, we asked him to pull over and "pop" the hood. He obliged.

The hood lifted - we were shocked: A "monster" engine with chromed valve covers. On the large snorkel air cleaner it read..."396 Turbo Jet. 325 HP."

325 horsepower? This thing ran like 500 hp - looking as if it could've powered a private cruise ship.

The Impala driver seemed nonchalant - saying casually - "I just got it from State Chevrolet. I'm still learning how to drive a stick."

Johnny was mortified; the only time I EVER saw him look worried.

What if I decided to "discuss" his loss at school on Monday? (i.e.) be a tattle tale.

Instantly, Johnnie realized that his fate rested in my hands. His stellar reputation - now ruined! Losing to an Impala would be completely devastating! Johnnie ridiculed unmercifully for weeks...even months. His pride destroyed.

Even worse, no longer would he be considered a Red Barn celebrity! But me, a TATTLE TALE? Nope, not my style. (i.e.) "Do unto others as you would have them do unto you."

Yes. I could indeed put myself in Johnnie's shoes:

FLASHBACK: October 1964.

It was Sunday night:

Dwight Patterson and I were on Market street; after watching a movie at the Boardman Plaza theater.

Then, a blue 64 SS 327 Impala pulled alongside us: two arrogant passengers (mid-20s) aboard - looking over like two smart azzes; as if saying..."let's go!"

Said Dwight :"Well Ricky, are you gonna race them?"

"DANG it." The very LAST thing I needed was to race ANOTHER 327 4-speed SS Impala - having been blown away by a 327 SS on Belmont last May.

The light went green, I thought...what the hell? Maybe I'd win for a change.

I floored the Bonneville!

The SS came screaming out of the hole, and blew me away. By at least 5 cars, maybe more!

At the next red light, Dwight — riding shot gun- had become buddy-buddy with the two guys in the SS; who now were laughing like hyenas. They were bantering back and forth.

After they drove off, Dwight blithely told me..."those guys were running 250 horses in that 327."

"You sure." Yes, Dwight was sure.

Fateful words indeed:

Next day (Monday) I was in 2nd period English, when Donny Tobin - who sat behind me - tapped me on my shoulder and whispered..."Hey, man, I heard your 389 Bonneville got blown away by a 327 250...ha ha."

WHAT?

Evidently, Dwight had been playing "town crier" - riding in on the early 8 AM school bus..."Hear ye, hear ye. Sandine's 389 Bonneville was blown away by a 327 SS, with 250 hp."

Immediately, the story began to spread, like a tidal wave rolling over the coastline.

Then in first period lunch, they were coming up to me - gleefully saying..."Hey Sandine. We heard your 389 Bonneville got blown away by a 327, 250 horse S... ha-ha...your Bonneville's a pig," etc.

How embarrassing! Most SS Impalas were 327 - 300 horses; but 250 horse power was the standard 327 engine in 64.

I thought..."that damm Dwight" - supposedly my great friend - had become Judas Iscariot (play Beatles "Hey Jude") happily telling EVERYONE about my losing to a 250 horse S 327.

Dwight, of course, had chosen to subordinate our friendship, in favor of maintaining his "image" around school: (i.e.) the one with all the "latest juicy gossip," etc.

Now at lunch, I had to avoid the cafeteria - getting food from vending machines near the gym. But that's what I got for bragging that a 389 Pontiac was the best engine...better than a Chevy...etc.

And now, in a remarkably similar situation with Johnny, I could either be a turncoat like Dwight Patterson or a TRUE friend Regarding Johnnie as a genuine friend. I said reassuringly...Johnnie, I'll them all that you DESTROYED that SS by four cars." Instantly, Johnnie lit up!- acting like a murder suspect who's just been pronounced NOT GUILTY: He was ELATED- freed from all anxiety! I'd made a friend for life.

I always knew it best to keep secrets among friends: they trusted me implicitly. After all, what's more important in life than a TRUE friend?

Nevertheless, street racing had forever changed: Chevrolet's new 396 "rat" motor would prove a game changer. It hit the streets unannounced.... a newly-unleashed secret weapon- aimed precisely at Pontiac's GTO.

It was late - getting dusk. Johnnie pulled into my driveway: "See ya tomorrow at lunch Sandy....stop over anytime...we'll shoot some pool."

Chapter 5

A '65 Catalina

Summer 1965:

Undoubtedly, Red Barn's most talked-about celebrity was the ever mysterious Davy Schultz - driving his splendid, midnight-blue 65 Pontiac Catalina: A drop-dead gorgeous car I would say.

And WOW, was it ever FAST - a heat-seeking missile on 4 wheels!

Davy Schultz was like "the Serial Killer" prowling Belmont: WARNING. Don't ever be caught at a red light next to him!

Davy's killer Pontiac was the fastest car anywhere around. But who REALLY was Davy Schultz? I had no idea at all.

By virtue of his amazingly fast Catalina, everyone knew about his car. But what about the man behind the wheel? Because he chose to be a "lone wolf," no one really knew anything about him. Schultz was like the "Lone Ranger" without the mask: "Who is that quiet guy that keeps blowing everyone away in that 2-door 65 Pontiac?"

Driving his super-tuned Pontiac, with his nonpareil ability with a 4-speed- Schultz was like James Bond wheeling his Aston Martin - leaving EVERYONE in the dust.

Davy and his car were ROCK STARS! Red Barn's most stellar attraction.

Schultz - despite his "celebrity" status - seemed to prefer being ALONE behind the wheel. Ergo, he'd never had anyone riding shotgun. And for some mysterious reason - no ladies riding beside him.

A true "lone wolf" he was indeed. (watch out for a full moon)

I was bewildered: Why Schultz shunned "companions" (girls) when they ALL wanted to ride in his beautiful, lightning-quick Pontiac.

Now, If it were ME driving a super-duper, gorgeous, 65 Catalina 4-speed: Man, I'd be lighting cigars with 20-dollar bills! - blowing kisses to all the LADIES - playing the role of "BIG MAN around TOWN!"

But Davy continued to shun his notoriety - preferring his beloved Pontiac to remain center stage. That was his game: the more mysterious, the better.

Indeed, the word around town was... "You don't P**S into the wind...and you don't DARE go up against Mr. Quick-Shift" Davy Schultz.

Most amazing of all was the sheer SPEED of Schultz's freaky-fast Pontiac - running like he had a 100-mph tailwind! This kept everyone wondering..."Just what the hell lurks beneath the hood of that blue Catalina?"

Davy's 389 Catalina was a bone-stock, 325 horsepower 4 barrel, but ran MORE like 425 horses! A factory-freak SCREAMER!

I regarded it as a "show car" because in a race, Schultz would SHOW you his tailights - pulling rapidly AWAY: a nightmare for anyone who's ever raced from a stop light.

With everyone bragging..."My car ain't never been beat," many would swallow those words after facing Davy Schultz.

Schultz was about 22 and not a bad-looking guy, but always by himself. Go figure.

With that rocket-fast car, who wouldn't want a ride? I sure would. Imagine the fun. The thrill. The excitement - riding in "the fastest car around!"

Drive a REALLY fast car? BOOM...instant rock star fame. WHY? Because a really fast car delivered incredible FUN...plus EXCITEMENT.

Ask yourself: Why do people wait incessantly in long lines at Kennywood, Six Flags, Cedar Point, etc., to ride the fastest coasters in the park? (patience is a virtue)

Because speed and neck-snapping acceleration are perceived as FUN. (i.e.) Going FAST is a BLAST! That's why people buy sports cars - because dago really fast!

Coasters are breathtaking, heart-pumping adventures, but without any underlying danger... "Look, Mom. No hands!"

Think about it: who among us doesn't find a thrill in going REALLY FAST?

It's all a part of our human nature.

Indeed, for all mankind - from time immemorial to the present - being "THE FASTEST" in anything meant EVERYTHING: for example:

- the world's fastest human.

- the fastest man on the football team

- the fastest car on the race track

- fastest swimmer in the NCAA

- the fastest skier in the downhill.

- fastest player in the major leagues

- the fastest worker on the assembly line.

- fastest mechanic in the shop

- the fastest grocery bagger in the supermarket

- fastest cone twirler at Dairy Queen...

- fastest dishwasher in the restaurant...

- fastest skater in Roller Derby

- the fastest sprinter on the track team

- fastest worker in the factory

- the fastest roofer in the crew-fastest seamstress in the shirt factory

- the fastest cop on the police force.

- the pitcher with the fastest fastball

- fastest ship in the Navy

- the fastest sorter in the mail room.

- the fastest lumberjack up a tree...

- fastest speedskater in the Olympics

- the fastest bartender in the nightclub

- fastest hot dog eater at a Nathan's contest

- the fastest waiter in the restaurant

- the fastest line cook in the kitchen

- the fastest bricklayer in the crew

- fastest hygienist in the dental clinic

- fastest cat in the jungle

- the tennis player with the fastest first-serve

- fastest greyhound at the dog track

- the fastest horse in the sweepstakes.

- fastest welder in the plant

- the fastest card dealer in the casino

- fastest bike rider in the Tour de France

- the fastest coaster in the amusement park

- the fastest typist in the office...

fastest delivery person in the pizza shop

- the fastest stocker on the grocery shelves

- the fastest loader on the dock.

- the fastest car in the 1/4 mile.

- fastest computer programmer...

- fastest runner in the Marathon

- the fastest cashier in the bank

- the fastest rower in the Ivy League

ETCETERA:

Bottom line: if you're the fastest in anything - no matter what - you were respected, well known; and probably earned the most money- plus job security.

Fame - and possibly fortune - usually are forthcoming if you're the FASTEST:

Remember the old western movies and TV shows from the 40s, 50s, and 60s? It was all about being the "FASTEST GUN AROUND."

The storyline was often predicated upon some hero cowboy, some desperado outlaw, or a law enforcement officer, ALL of whom were known as the FASTEST!

Yeah, that adjective "FASTEST." Does it not evoke thrills....excitement...entertainment...and FUN?

Americans love (and worship) just about anything FAST!

Think about it: Would you rather watch "Fast Gun Sheriff Wyatt Earp," or "The Story of Homer Filby" from Clodhopper,

Missoura: the docile old cowpoke who wasn't even allowed to carry a gun.

In America - in particular- the mystique of speed was an underlying factor on why the United States emerged in the late 19th century, as the greatest nation on Earth.

We Americans became the great country that we are, because our role models were always the fastest; or the smartest people to be found.

So no wonder why Davy Schultz was held in such awesome regard. His Catalina was the fastest car around!

Another HUGE benefit of driving a "big time" muscle car: LADIES noticed: they craved the excitement. (i.e.) "Girls just wanna have fun" (play Cindy Lauper song).

To drive a fast car meant instant fame within one's circle of friends. Hence, a former "nobody" now became "somebody"... just by virtue of driving a sleek, beautiful muscle car.

Now began a new "social revolution."

In times BEFORE muscle cars, the only way one could impress the most desirable girls in school - cheerleaders... majorettes... prom queens - was to be some macho, bad-azz TOUGH guy (i.e.) "I don't take NO shet from NOBODY." (duh)

Or...if you were a STARTER (first string) on the football or basketball team; or perhaps, a golden gloves boxer.

All others need not apply.

But now, in the mid-1960s, ANY nurd in school suddenly became "popular," AFTER Daddy co-signed for his new, SS 327 4-

speed Malibu convertible. Instantly, he's ACCEPTED into all the best "cliques." (no more more sitting alone during lunch).

Not surprisingly, sales of all "muscle" cars began burgeoning all across the USA. It was PURE mania! And why not? What was more fun than laying a molten strip of burning rubber?

Seems that everyone that could afford one, went out and bought a big V8 muscle car. They were in HUGE demand.

I remember helping Dad with the lawn one Saturday afternoon: Then, at the 4-way stop (up the block) a white 4-speed, 65 GTO was turning left- going by our house - giving a loud chirp from his rear tires as hit second (gear).

Dad - amazed - staring at the GTO said..."Wow, look at the red-line tires on that thing! So that's this GTO you keep talking about? Sharp car!"

I said...."I told you Dad! Let's trade in the Bonneville! You can fit 5 people in a GTO."

Dad laughed; but at least he now knew why I'd gone completely loco about getting a 65 GTO.

Street racing became a nationwide PARTICIPATION sport. Smoking the rear tires gave one a sense of power. Even better, it drew everyone's attention.

Added to the suspense of a street race was the nervous anticipation at a red light between two drivers. How many horses were under the other guy's hood?

The closer the light was to changing green, the more your pulse would pound..."Hope I don't get blown away."

Such incredible suspense - waiting at red lights.

And if you won...YEAH MAN... you felt elated! You could brag forever to EVERYONE about the guy you'd just blown away in your 63 327 Impala. (i.e) Something "you could tell to your grandchildren."

I remember, when I was playing golf - June '64: I'd hooked my errant tee shot out by the street; and when bending over to pick up my ball, came this incredibly loud "G-R-R-O-O-O-O-O-O-OM." SO LOUD! It was an aquamarine 64 GTO zooming by: its tripower carbs WAILING like thunder.

WOW!

Most amazing and impressive sound I'd ever heard! With its high compression 389 and triple two-barrel carburetors, a tripower GTO had a thundering sound you'd never forget.

Like dinosaurs?

I prefer to call the tri-power 65 GTO the Tyrannosaurus Rex of all muscle cars- roaming the asphalt jungle...looking to eat up a hapless 327 Chevy, Cutlass 442, or a 383 Dodge Coronet.

A tripower GTO was world champion for scorching tires! Uniroyal couldn't roll out those red lines fast enough.

Red Barn - per capita- saw more rubber burned than anywhere on Earth! You could smell it from a distance. A pall of blue tire smoke hung in the air.

Drive through Red Barn in a hot car, everyone would point and yell..."Light up those tires!"..."GO MAN GO!"

The nightly pandemonium at Red Barn began causing traffic jams on Belmont; from the parade of cars waiting to pull in. It literally was a drawing card for all show-offs in

their muscle cars.

It was the mid-'60s. When life was actually fun! With fast cars, rock/soul music, drag racing, and cheeseburgers. It was the "Leave It To Beaver" era - the very epitome of family life in the mid-60s America.

Mad Magazine's Alfred E. Neuman said it best..."What? Me Worry?"

Red Barn's parking lot now became like an old wild West town: Muscle car "shoot outs" occurring at any time; and on any night.

A hot car would enter Red Barn - its driver looking for the fastest car in the parking lot. Then came the obligatory showdown on Belmont...DRAW! (i.e.) "READY...GET SET...GO."

And careful where you PARKED:

The celebrity guys had their own "personal" parking spots, where only THEY could park.

Jackie Stevens' tri-power black 65 GTO, would be in 'his' spot, by the front lot entrance; and always with hood open, so you'd see those ultra cool, triple two barrel carbs.

Parked near the restaurant's side entrance was the "GTO Killer" (i.e.) Greg Spector's gorgeous white 65 Malibu SS 4-speed: hood open (of course) so you could get a look-see at his L-79 327 cube, 350 hp engine: one of the fastest cars in town.

In the back row: Vic Funkhouser's sleek, red, fastback 65 Mustang GT; with its "289 High Performance" fender badges. This undoubtedly was one of the best looking muscle cars of all time; and it stood out vs. all the other cars on the lot.

"Wanted. Security guard. Apply within. Must be 21."

Working as a rent-a-cop at Red Barn was not exactly a "career position." Most lasted but a few weeks (i.e.) rent - don't buy- the uniform.

Many security guards quickly would assume an exaggerated sense of self-importance - like they were J. Edgar Hoover - hunting down a Red Barn "common criminal" for the "capital offense" of burning rubber (i.e.) "disturbing the peace."

But since Red Barn would only hire ONE guard at a time to "police" the huge parking lot, a newly-hired security guard became much like a hapless lion tamer - faced with too many wild lions at once! And soon would follow yet another "premature resignation" from a flabbergasted, "distressed" rent-a-cop (sorry: no gold watch)

And the girls! Every night at Red Barn was (oh yes) "Ladies Night." (play Kool 'n the Gang song)

Females galore - driving daddy's car - packed full with 4- 5, or even 6 chicks. Eager to meet some hot shot driving a Corvette, GTO; or an SS Malibu - flirting with anyone who drove an appealing car.

Imagine: AM car radios blaring to the iconic hits of the 60's; undoubtedly the best music of all time; with everyone grooving to Motown, the British invasion; and all the talented "girl groups."

"Let the good times roll!"

Another strange thing - for some IDIOTIC reason- drivers would display pointless, irrelevant decals on their cars.

One of the more popular ones read... "Hooker Headers." Headers? How stupid! Who even knew what a header was?

Also the decal "STP" (oil additive) was often seen. Seemed incredibly STUPID to me. Who the hell cared about what kind of OIL you used?

Davy Schultz- being the ultimate Pontiac man - proudly displayed two large blue and red decals on his Catalina's rear windows - saying..."Genuine Pontiac Parts."

I wondered: What OTHER parts could there POSSIBLY be? Buick parts? Mercury parts? Jeep? Alfa Romeo? Fiat? So totally redundant!

Other drivers did likewise: whatever it took to be noticed.

Tony Tarantino - driving his 65 Galaxy - had "Genuine Ford Parts" on his back windows. Eric Kutsko - driving his 55 Chevy - had (you guessed it) "Genuine Chevrolet Parts" on his windows, etc.

Another "head scratcher." How did the Red Barn continue to stay in business? I wondered. Despite throngs of cars/people outside in the parking lot, ACTUAL paying customers going inside were few and far between.

At night - outside the restaurant - one could hear shouting. Laughter. People milling about - leaning on vehicles. Hoods open. Radios blaring. Cars burning rubber - laying strips. Greasers arguing/congregating.

But walk inside - where was everyone? No need to pick a number. You were "next."

The counter was usually deserted. Empty tables. Cash registers not ringing. Employees yawning...daydreaming.

Not exactly the place to enjoy "five-star dining." (wine list not available)

Quality wise, Red Barn's burgers approached McDonalds; but soggy, cold (ugh) french fries proved disastrous - the perfect "unhappy meal."

And don't even bother with the hot apple pie...It was COLD.

By August, Davy Schultz's reputation began spreading far and wide.

Word was that some "bad boy" in an L-78 Corvette was coming down from Warren (OH) - about 13 miles away- to challenge Schultz this coming Friday at midnight.

L-78 Corvettes were "new on the block" - a fearsome, 396 cubic inch "rat" motor, with 11-1 compression, solid lifter camshaft - officially rated at 425 hp: but it was probably closer to 475/500 hp.

L-78s were so LOUD! You could literally FEEL the pavement vibrate when one went driving by.

Throughout that next week, anticipation at Red Barn was not unlike waiting for a heavyweight title fight. Was Davy Schultz - the automotive Caesar of Red Barn- about to surrender his scepter and crown?

Finally... Friday night - parking lot jammed. Everyone waiting for this fire-breathing, dragon-slaying L-78 vette to make its appearance.

After MIDNIGHT it was apparent: the L-78 Corvette had dogged out- not wanting to finish second a street race; the ultimate humiliation in front of a crowd.

Good thing Mr. L-78 never showed up. Schultz would've shown him his tail lights. These big bad 396 corvettes could be uncontrolled monsters when coming out of the hole - fishtailing and wheel-hopping sideways.

Way too much power for a small, fiberglass corvette. (less is more).

So if you "messed up with your clutch, you'd be "standing there" - frying away your back tires; while your opponent is happily pulling away- waving bye-bye!"

By summer of 66, a shocking mystery had descended upon Red Barn: Davy Schultz- and his iconic Pontiac Catalina - seemed to have disappeared off the face of the earth.

Never again was Schultz and Catalina seen at Red Barn.... the proverbial "one year wonder."

Nevertheless, the Schultz legend lives on:

Perhaps he'd driven off into the sunset - like an old western cowboy hero - never looking back.

It was just like that late-60's Rolling Stones song: the indomitable Davy Schultz was truly one helluva "STREET FIGHTIN' MAN."

Chapter 6

A '65 GTO

JUNE 1965:

I was at home in the kitchen on a hot sunny day in late June when I heard a car pull into the driveway:

I could not believe my eyes! A fantastic-looking, **LIPSTICK RED** '65 GTO was now standing in the driveway before me, with my **FAVORITE** cousin, Mona, behind the wheel. She was a year older than me.

I was **FLOORED**! - *I NEARLY fainted!* (holy mackerel)

ME: *"Mona! When did you get THAT?"* (new GTO)

MONA: *"My father bought it for my (high school) graduation present...Is Aunt Debbie home?"*

(Mona walked in)

Oh boy! Whenever Mom and Mona would get together for a *"cordial family chat,"* they became the *"Dynamic Duo"*-blabbing happily away with each other for hours!

Another epic yakety-yak marathon was at hand!

Mona and I had been "best friend cousins" since we were little kids:

We'd always had fun together - especially at family birthday parties:

All our cousins would be there!

We'd pair off and have a blast! - playing Hide 'n Go Seek. Red Rover. Card games. Water fights. Chutes 'n Ladders. Sand box. Old Maid. Chinese Checkers. Roller skates.Tag. Mr. Potato Head. Cootie. Hopscotch. Squirt guns. Hula hoops. The Slinky. Whiffle ball, etc.

Things kids liked to do in the 1950s (back in the "Leave it to Beaver" days).

"HEY MOM...Mona's here! Hurry-up! Come out and say hello."

MOM: *"Oh hi Mona! How are you? Come in! Sit down! Are you hungry?"*

As I walked around looking at Mona's new GTO, I was stunned: it was as if this miraculously beautiful car had appeared out of nowhere and landed in the driveway in front of me.

Of course, the first priority was to check out what's under the hood. Wow, the classic Pontiac 389 V8; the same one in our

Bonneville, but with chromed valve covers, chromed oil dipstick, and a thin, flat (pancake) chrome air cleaner.

Indeed, if "CAR and DRIVER" magazine had a centerfold, Mona's GTO would be "Dream Car of the Month." It was jaw-droppingly beautiful! - how the overall lines of the GTO blended so perfectly together.

It was that oh-so-cool, sleek, bulging hood scoop: It made the GTO look like a tiger was lurking beneath the hood...GRRRR.

Next: A distinctive logo! (GTO 6.5 liter) behind the front wheel wells: A car with its own logo? Pure class! Just like a Ferrari.

Pontiac had leap-frogged the boundaries of COOL!

Such style! Such class and this was designed to be a *"muscle"* car?

The stacked vertical headlights and blacked-out grill gave the car that menacing yet elegant look that only Pontiac could have imagined. It was just plain breathtakingly beautiful.

Down its side ran a black *"accent"* pinstripe - totally cool!

The GTO's angular roofline matched up perfectly with the overall contour of the car. Sharp. Absolutely beautiful!

The black interior was breathtaking. Functional. Beautiful. Perfect: The dashboard was simple - yet elegant. Even the floor mats were impressive.

The GTO's size was perfect. Not massive, like our Bonneville...and not small, like Aunt Catherine's crummy little Nash Rambler.

I kept walking around the GTO - shaking my head in wonder-thinking..."Wow; NO WAY could they ever improve upon the way this GTO looked! It was almost "too perfect." (as time progressed, I'd be proven correct)

Seems that Pontiac's **DESIGN** engineers had hit a grand-slam home run! The 65 GTO - to me - was the best-looking American car of all time! Perfect-looking from any aspect.

Little did I know that, in a minute, my life would be changed...forever.

At the kitchen table, I heard Mom..."*Mona, would you like something to drink?*"

"*Umm, do you have any Coke or ginger ale?*"

Opening the fridge, Mom shrieked... "*Who drank all the pop? Hurry up! Run up to the store and get something for Mona...get my purse!*"

After Mom gave me money and the keys, I said, "Mona, could you move your car?"

"Oh, just take mine," she said nonchalantly while opening her purse - handing me her keys.

Lucky me! For ONCE in my life, I was in the right place at the right time - driving Mona's new 65 goat! I was trying to conceal my excitement!

Opening the GTO's door...my pulse was pounding..."*Am I dreaming...is this really happening?*"

Sitting behind the wheel, my left hand was shaking so excessively I could barely insert the ignition key. I was never so nervous in my life.

Then, It started up with a booming.

"WHA-ROOOOOOOOOM!"

WOW: Instantly, I felt this surge of *"potential energy"* - coming right through the steering wheel in my hands. A beast was about to be let loose onto the streets!

It was a seminal moment in my life - never having experienced such a sensation of extraordinary power that I knew was lurking under this GTO's hood.

Even more amazing: after backing out, a mere TAP on the gas produced a distinctive *"chirp"* (two-speed automatic transmission) from the back tires!

A car that could CHIRP the rear tires? - after BARELY touching the gas? Immediately, I sensed this would be a total blast - driving a car that was super FAST- compared to our gigantic Bonneville.

Spur-of-the-moment I detoured to Frankie Malone's house. I knew he'd be home.

Frank came rushing out - eyes huge with astonishment.

"Wow...where did you get THAT?"

"Hurry...get in...we haven't got much time!"

The beverage store was near the Dairy Queen on Belmont...a place always *"mobbed"* on a hot summer day.

Pulling into the crowded DQ parking lot, it was just like an

old EF Hutton TV commercial: instantly, everyone FROZE in their tracks - riveted by Mona's stunning GTO - unbelieving of what their eyes told them.

One could NOT imagine a better-looking car than Mona's bright red, super-sleek GTO!

I felt like a star driving through the parking lot: an instant celebrity!

Everyone was pointing excitedly as we rolled by.

"Wow! Nice car!"

"Look at that red goat!"

"Hey man, chirp out."

A blonde kid - about 10 - yelled..."*Let's see some rubber burn!"*

It was pure ELATION. Now I knew what it felt like to be KING! A fantasy come to life.

Showing off at McDonalds was next - a mile and a half up Belmont.

Driving the GTO, I was in another world; everyone giving me a *"thumbs up."*

Frank, instigating, said..."*C'mon, grampa, floor it! Let's go* **RACE** *someone."*

NO WAY! I knew a ticket or accident would be ruinous.

But knowing "maniac" Frank - he would keep up the instigating.

Just ahead was a busy intersection at Belmont and Gypsy Lane...a long red light.

A white, 65 Olds 442 was in the left lane - driven by this eerie-looking weirdo, about 22. - wearing cheap sunglasses: Something unnerved me about him. I knew he was *"itching"* for a street race (brilliant deduction).

"Weirdo" kept looking over at me menacingly - like he was the "Big-Bad Wolf." (i.e.) *"I'll huff...and I'll puff and blow your GOAT away!"*

I could hear *"I GOT YOU BABE"* by Sonny 'n Cher coming from his radio. Then he turned down the volume... a sure sign he was *"ready to race."*

What a conundrum: Either race this creep or play it safe. But then I'd never hear the END of it from Frank (i.e.) *"You're a BIG chicken-shet."* (he was like that)

Just as the light turned green, a car ahead pulled out slowly onto Belmont from the Sohio gas station. Then, it turned down a side street.

The road ahead was now CLEAR: *"Creepo"* beside me in the left lane. Frank was nearly delirious, yelling...*"Race him! Blow his doors off!"* **GO**!

But racing on Belmont at high noon? The speedometer said 35 mph. I was looking for cops in my mirror.

Frank kept egging me. The 442 weirdo was looking over at me from the left lane.

I figured... *"just GO for it:"*

I mashed the gas pedal to the floor! Oh my god! It was like dumping gasoline on a bonfire!

"GRRRRRRROOOOOOOOOOOOOOOOOOM!"

The GTO roared like thunder...front end violently leaping upward!

My head JERKED back...like being sucker-punched in the forehead!

Simultaneously, I heard a loud *"SCREEEEEECH"*- the GTO actually laying a FIVE foot strip! - plainly visible in my mirror.

It was mind-boggling! I actually got SCARED - such was the **FORCEFUL**, violent response FROM nailing the gas pedal. It was a thunderclap! Most amazing moment of my life!

Mona's GTO was so unbelievably FAST; our eyes were wide open with ASTONISHMENT!

Said Frank: *"Wow, can you believe this?"*

Looking in my mirror, the 442 weirdo was probably thinking, *"Wow"*.... trailing by at least five car lengths.

For me, it was a life-altering moment- NEVER to be forgotten!

A car that laid a 5-foot strip at 35 mph?

UNCANNY! Amazing torque! Such blistering ACCELERATION - from the GTO's explosive, high-compression 389 engine.

Frank kept saying...*"This car is unbelievable..."* Your cousin's goat is unbelievable." "Unbelievable, how bad we beat that 442."* etc.

I headed for the carryout. No golden arches today. *"Time was of the essence."*

After dropping off Frank, I was thinking...*"What an incredibly FAST n' FUN car! God! I was on cloud nine!*

Walking into the house, it was as though I'd crashed the 8th inning of the *"World Series of Gossip."* Mom 'n Mona ignored me- completely.

They were blithely discussing Aunt Mary's heated argument with Aunt Helen; and how Mom had seen Uncle Bill *"dressed like a bum"* at the grocery store, etc.

I put the pop into the fridge.

Spur of the moment, I then decided to "tidy up" Mona's GTO. I cleaned the asphalt splatter off the rocker panels, then I washed off all the dust and road grime.

While brushing out the interior, I kept wishing...*"WHY couldn't this car be mine?"* Imagine - driving a 65 GTO! What could exceed THAT?

The excitement. The envy! Girls around the car - imploring me to take them for a ride!

And then the RED BARN! My friends would DIE seeing me there - in a new 65 GTO!

I was still in mild shock - words couldn't describe that moment. I knew my life had been forever changed.

Never could I forget that overwhelming adrenaline rush! The indisputable, most thrilling-exciting experience of my life - encapsulated into 45 minutes.

Then - for no apparent reason - I remembered being a 5th grader, and the first time I ever watched "Twilight Zone" on a Friday night.

Rod Serling's opening narration could have been adapted to the 65 GTO:

QUOTE: *"You're traveling through another dimension, a dimension not only of sight and sound but of VELOCITY and ACCELERATION. Sheer speed on the street. A journey into a wondrous land whose boundaries are that of premium gasoline. That's the signpost up ahead - your next stop, the GTO Zone."*

Back in 1965, young farmers joined "4-H Clubs."

But 65 GTO owners had mythical "4-A" clubs:

-Astounding 389 high compression engine.

-Astounding beauty.

-Astonishing acceleration...GRRRRRRR.

-Astoundingly fun to drive.

A car like no other....before or SINCE!

When Mona saw her GTO, she was absolutely delighted: *"Wow, Rick, nice job..." "Thanx!"*

After Mona left, Mom retreated back to her bedroom to watch..."Another World" (her late afternoon soap opera).

Yeah. That sure "nailed" it for me:

During the surreal, 45 minute ride in Mona's amazing GTO, I too, had been in "another world." A twilight zone of unearthly excitement - never to be exceeded again.

A '65 GTO

Chapter 7

AUGUST 1965:

I was at Gray Drug store - thumbing through all latest car magazines. Naturally, I was looking for articles about "my true love" - the drop-dead gorgeous 65 GTO! Being so thoroughly obsessed - looking at pictures of a stunning 65 GTO bordered on "automotive porno." So CAPTIVATING. I just could not take away my eyes!

Ever since I was a kid (late 50's) I always noticed Pontiacs. One autumn day, I was riding my Schwinn bike; when I spotted this huge, new, shiny black 59 Bonneville in my neighbor's driveway. Wow!

Immediately, I stopped - "parked my bike" - and walked around this spectacular 2-door beauty. It looked amazing! The chrome. The grille. The tail lights. This car was an absolute jaw-dropper! (I still remember it)

Ever since the late 50's, Pontiac had boldly stepped forward, staying YEARS ahead of the competition. In their TV commercials, Pontiac always included... "all new." (e.g.) "See the ALL NEW WIDE-TRACK '59 Pontiac at your local Pontiac dealership."

Pontiac's styling was avant-garde. Bold. Outstanding. The leader in automotive trends. In 1963, Pontiac introduced "stacked" headlights. They looked phenomenal. Not surprisingly, copycat Ford came out with stacked headlights in 1965. Other car companies soon followed. Of course, who ELSE but Pontiac would inaugurate America's muscle car era with its iconic 1964 GTO.

NOTE: in 1964, the benchmark for a REALLY FAST car was zero to 60 in SIX seconds. But spring, 1964 - "Car and Driver" - zero to sixty - had clocked a

tripower 64 GTO in a mind-boggling 4.6 seconds! WHOA BABY!

This was equivalent to Mickey Mantle hitting 5 home runs in a single game - swinging from both sides of home plate.

Jim Brown - running for 400 yards in one game.

Wilt Chamberlain- scoring 125 points in one game.

Arnold Palmer - shooting 59 for 18 holes.

"Bullet" Bob Hayes - sprinting 100 meters in 9 flat.

Pele, scoring 10 goals in one soccer game.

Bill Rogers, running the marathon in 23 hours.

Joe DiMaggio - hitting consecutively in 80 games.

Willie Shoemaker- riding to 2 consecutive triple crowns.

I remember walking into my homeroom; and an excited Dwight

Patterson - showing me the "Car and Driver" article about the 64 tripower GTO - clocking that amazing 0-60 time...4.6 seconds.

Wow.

In their most recent issue, "MOTOR TREND" had chosen the ENTIRE 1965 Pontiac model line as "Cars of the Year."

65 Pontiacs took the USA car market by storm. Such ingenuity!

Such beauty! And fast!

YEAH: FAST! Americans have always loved fast cars.

Indeed; considering all the cumulative minutes a driver endures waiting at red lights: over a LIFETIME, it can add up to hundreds of hours - spent idling away at those ubiquitous traffic signals.

So why not be ready? - when some hot shot cretin — driving his 4-speed 327 Chevy - is about to embarrass you in your stodgy 61 Ford Galaxie.

Even worse: he's looking over at you with a provocative smirk -knowing you haven't got a Chinaman's chance upon the green light.

SOLUTION: You skedaddle on over to your friendly Pontiac

dealer...looking for a family car "with some balls."

Bye-bye, slowpoke '61 Galaxie. Hello '65 tripower Catalina!

By the mid-60s, Americans had become obsessed with racing from red lights. And here's Pontiac, with its fearsome, fabled GTO; and its vastly-improved 1965 389 engine; an engineering marvel.

Even better: In 65, Pontiac (GM) introduced its terrific, fast-shifting, "smooth-as-silk" 3-speed turbo-hydramatic transmission.

Not surprisingly, the 65 Catalina and Bonneville were exceeding all sales expectations. It was that new, sizzling-hot Pontiac 389 engine! A huge hit with the driving public.

Interestingly, "Car and Driver" said: QUOTE:

"Behind the wheel of a FULL-SIZED 65 Pontiac, you could AMBUSH an unsuspecting opponent from a red light."

(August 1965 edition).

One August Sunday afternoon, I was mowing the lawn when

Frankie Malone - driving a gorgeous, new, white 2-door 65

Bonneville - drives up to my yard...I flipped out!

"Frank! Where'd you get THAT new Bonneville?"

"It's my uncle Tony's new car. He let me have it for this afternoon..."

hurry up...get in!"

Frank turned right onto 5th Avenue and floored it: G-R-R-R-R-R-R-R-R-RO-O-M!

Wow! For a huge Bonneville, it accelerated like a gigantic GTO!

And it shifted so quickly and so smoothly! The all-new GM, 3-speed "turbo-hydramatic" was nothing short of phenomenal!

"Car and Driver" had been right on! This new Bonneville was a blast! It was luxurious and amazingly fast! I absolutely LOVED this car.

IMMEDIATELY, Frank headed out Market Street, looking for a street race; like a hungry lioness - prowling the Serengeti.

We had only gone 2 blocks up Market; when - coming from the opposite direction - we saw two 4-speed 65 SS Impalas - deadlocked in a loud, pulse-pounding street race!

A '65 Impala SS

VAR-O-O-O-O-OOM!

The two Impalas - side by side - were running DEAD EVEN!

As they went roaring away in the opposite direction, Frank and I looked at each other...saying, "WOW...did you see that?"

For two die-hard street-racing lunatics, it was pure euphoria!

Think about it: a hot, summer Sunday afternoon:

A young man might be watching baseball. Playing softball. Golfing. Swimming. Camping. Tennis. At an amusement park Doing yard work. Relaxing on the front porch. Getting tanned at the beach. Waxing the car. Shooting baskets. Home repairs. Walking the dog. Cleaning out the garage: whatever.

But in Youngstown? Nope! If one had a fast car, it was head on out to Market street and "run whatcha brung." (play Bruce Springsteen "Baby We Were Born to Run").

Suddenly, a gold 65 442 goes zooming by us in the opposite direction. Without hesitation, Frank made a U-turn. We were both dying with anticipation; about to race a bad-azz 442!

A '65 442

At the next red light, we pulled up next to this beautiful 442. Driver was in his mid-20s; with a shaved head. Big biceps. Gruff facial expression. Probably a military type, headed for Vietnam: or maybe in the National Guard.

Although he appeared macho, he acted rather perverse (a weirdo).

For one thing, the Olds 442 - being new for 65 - meant all 442 drivers felt they had "something to prove." Hence, they'd race ANYONE at a red light. But NOT this bozo next to us. Light changes: Frank goes tearing away from the green light! Shockingly, the 442 lagged way behind...wouldn't race!

Frank was incensed - yelling over..."Are you some kinda chicken?"

Feigning laughter, Mr. 442 arrogantly replied..."Ha-ha-ha...I wouldn't waste my time on that AIRCRAFT CARRIER."

Hardy-har... a real comedian.

I looked over at his 442. It sounded imposing. Its 4-speed gears whining away: dual exhaust pipes loudly rumbling. So why was he backing off?

From one red light to the next, Frank played provocateur: "C'mon man! Something wrong with that 442?"..."You just learning how to drive a stick? Thinking about driver training?" etc.

I wondered...EVERY 65 442 personally known to me was plenty fast. SO WHY would this gashole not race?

FLASHBACK: Around 4th of July; a month earlier: I saw Colin

Blakely - driving a new black, 65 442 - pulling into the Red Barn.

After cruising around the lot, he turned right...and nailing the gas pedal, he went streaking up Belmont - his tail lights disappearing so incredibly quickly. It left me stunned! It was blistering FAST!

A '65 Impala SS Convertible

FLASHBACK: May 1965; a Sunday afternoon. Frankie and I were at Isaly's - where all the north side greasers would hang out.

Just then, from the nearby 4-way stop, I heard "WOOLY BULLY" by Sam the Sham - playing over a car radio.

It was Ralph Bartolo - radio blasting away. He lived nearby – driving his new, red 65 442. Everyone stared at his impressive car. Once all eyes were upon him, Bartolo rolled halfway into the intersection; then NAILED the gas!

V-R-R-R-OOOOOOOOM! He went blazing down Ohio Ave like Haley's comet! Wow. Give that man a cigar! Bartolo's 442 was one really FAST mother-brother! It soon became known as "the quickest car on the North side."

FLASHBACK- April '65: I was eating lunch in the high school cafeteria. sitting at my table was Bob Stankovich; who drove a burgundy 65 GTO, 4-barrel 4-speed. Seems that Bobby was thinking twice about racing some west side rival, who'd challenged him- driving through Burger Chef.

It was Kenny Thomas - driving a parchment (white) 65 442. The terror of the west side! A car that had never been beat.

Not surprisingly, Stankovich "chickened out"- never lining up against Thomas and his intimidating 442. But who could blame him?

FLASHBACK: December 1964: We were EIGHT guys, joyriding out Market Street - in Freddy Sniderman's gigantic, 1958 Olds 98...a rusty old "beater" car. We were ridin' in style!

Radio blasting - we all were singing merrily along to..."You've Lost That Lovin Feeling" (Righteous Brothers); when ZOOM-

WHOOM; a black 65 GT Mustang fastback, and a yellow 65 442, went streaking by us in the right lane - lining up at the next red light - directly in front of us.

Instantly, we rolled down the windows...all EXCITED – listening anxiously to the loud revving of engines, coming from both cars.

Then, a shocking surprise: Light changes, and "VAR-ROOOOOOM," the 442 streaked away, like an unleashed bottle rocket!

We all looked at each other - saying..."WOW! Did you see THAT?"

The Mustang GT had lost by at least 6 car lengths: This devastating 442 ran like it had "thunder & lightning" beneath its hood! God, was it ever FAST! Presently, we remained side-by-side with this mysterious 442 goon; who seemed to relish Frank's verbal abuse: Chatter had now become openly belligerent: Insults going back 'n forth: it was like being in 8th grade again - watching a "cut down fight" during recess.

I kept wondering: "Who - driving a fast car - would be on Market Street on a Sunday afternoon? - UNLESS they were looking for a street race."

Even worse: Why was a single man not at Mom 'n Dad's house? - which is where virtually all unmarried men could be found on a Sunday. Conceivably, even his own mother and father didn't like him.

Couldn't imagine him having ANY lady friends...perhaps NO friends at all. He was probably a loner since childhood - who always sat by himself during lunch at school. (you know the type). In class, the kid who'd always get sick - puking all over the floor.

On Valentine's Day; no girl wanted him to be "her Valentine." At recess, the hapless one, who (unknowingly) would bear a "KICK ME" sign that someone had blithely taped onto his back: (poor soul)

Even stranger: Although alone, he was not listening to the car's radio.Then...ALERT!

We were stopped at the last red light before the Market street bridge: As it was about to go green, this mysterious buffoon now sat UPRIGHT in his seat - a sudden change in posture: His arrogant facial expression now reflected anxiety (uncertainty).

Obviously, the sudden change in his body language said this 442 driver was indeed, gettin' ready to race us! I warned Frank; but he'd been EXPECTING this joker to pull such a shenanigan.

The light jumped green! Both the 442 and Frank came storming out of the "chute"...almost dead even! The 442 ahead, by not even a fender (3 feet).

He was turning pale- absolutely shocked! We remained "right there"- right beside him! Incredibly, all across the long Market Street bridge, the 442 could not pull away. Frank was determined...trying his utmost to win! What an unbelievably close race! - ending in with the 442, only 3 feet ahead.

At the red light downtown, Mr. 442 - now amazed - asked..."What the hell's in that Bonneville? Is it tri-power?" Frank was laughing - immensely pleased with himself.

What a stunning turn of events! A massive, two-ton 65 Bonneville...running even with a 3,200 lb. 65 442! What were the odds on that ever happening?

A '65 Bonneville

Think about it: we'd come within 3 feet of pulling off a great upset! Like Joe Namath & his '68 Jets vs. the over-confident Baltimore Colts in the 1969 Super Bowl: Or Arthur Ashe - whipping that cretin Jimmie Connors - in the 1975 Wimbledon finals. Incredibly, "Car and Driver" magazine had predicted it all along: QUOTE:

"Behind the wheel of a of a FULL-SIZED 65 Pontiac, you could ambush an unsuspecting opponent from a red light."

A full-sized, 65 Pontiac - with its factory 389, four barrel (325 hp); would easily surprise many an unsuspecting driver at red lights.

What was more fun than embarrassing a 327 Corvette; or a 383 Mopar, in your big, beautiful, 65 Catalina? Hence, 2-door 65 Pontiac Catalinas seldom ever go on sale in classic car magazines.

Today, a 2-door 65 Catalina in your garage is like "money in the bank." It's just like real estate land: (i.e.) "they ain't making any **MORE."**

Chapter 8

AUGUST 1965:

The 65 PONTIAC GTO had become a nationwide SENSATION.

American drivers were clamoring to hear Pontiac's GTO TIGER - growling under their hoods!

By summer '65 Pontiac dealers had a 2 month waiting list. Demand for the 65 GTO had far exceeded the supply.

And why not? What was more fun than wheeling around town in a jaw-dropping, tire-scorching, head-snapping 65 GTO!

In my opinion, the 65 GTO was America's first ELECTRIC car; the way it jolted American culture and society; so much so, that acquiring a 'muscle car' had become a nationwide obsession.

Americans love speed. Going FAST. A nation of movers and achievers. Hence, our dialect reflects as much: "Get moving! Hurry UP! Lets GO! Get a move on! Let's HIGHTAIL it! Get the LEAD OUT! Get your rear in GEAR! DOUBLE TIME!"

"C'MON, STEP ON IT!"

Yeah...STEP ON IT! It's here where the 65 GTO became legendary.

There was no greater excitement than stomping on the gas in a 65 GTO!

G-R-R-R-R-R-ROOOOOOOOOOM!

The front end jumped up like a wild horse! The amazingly powerful 389 engine went off like a stick of dynamite! VAR-ROOOOOOOOOM.

Your head would jerk back; like running into a clothesline! Wow. Everyone pointing..."Look at that GTO go!"

Burning rubber? The 65 GTO was world champion! Uniroyal couldn't crank-out red line tires fast enough. Pontiac - branding the car as the "GEETO Tiger" - had cleverly implanted MACHO into its message (i.e.) a tiger - the most revered animal of all - was lurking under your hood; and YOU were its master.

The 65 GTO - with its dazzling acceleration - truly was like "having a tiger by the tail." Pontiac's 65 GTO was on a roll- everywhere: There were GTO songs. GTO Magazines. 45 RPM records. Slogans. GTO contests. Tee shirts...first prize drawings, etc.

Even Thom McCan jumped into the craze - introducing "GTO shoes." GTO SHOES? Seriously? WHAT next? Cadillac underwear? Chevrolet socks? Buick belts? Oldsmobile gloves?

September 1965:

It was my first week back at high school: (my senior year) At first period lunch, Dwight Patterson came up to me - flashing a magazine ad about GTO shoes.

Plan was, Dwight and I would - after school - walk downtown to visit "Thom McCann Shoes" on W. Federal street.

The store was dumpy. Dusty. Dingy. Burned out fluorescent lights in the ceiling. Utterly DRAB! I wanted to leave; but "trend-setter" Dwight seemed dead-set on getting a pair of insipid "GTO" shoes. The young shoe clerk - wearing his polyester "perma-press" white shirt - was very polite. After Dwight tried on the first pair - wrong size. Whispering, I said..."Dwight...do NOT buy those ugly PUERTO-RICAN shoes!" (a racist slur). The shoes had tacky, slanted heels - with "GTO" imprinted upon the back. So ugly! And pricey! Naturally, GTO shoes, nationwide, were a total bust.

Thom McCan shoe store eventually went under - deservedly so. Problem was - with summer ending - no more 65 GTO: What would the 66 GTO look like? I shuddered to even entertain such disquieting thoughts.

How could Pontiac possibly improve upon the 65 GTO?- a car that ALREADY looked beautifully perfect, and ran like a champion.

FINALLY: revelation day: Pontiac announced September 27,1965, the all-new 66 Pontiac line of cars would be publicly revealed. Ergo, Dwight and I would go to Valley Pontiac - only a block away - and see the new 66 GTO.

FLASHBACK: 1957- back when I was in 3rd grade: Dad called me into our living room. He was actually quite excited! He showed me a newspaper article - featuring the all-new 58 Edsel. Dad always loved Fords - fondly remembering his teen-age days - driving his 36 Ford 2-door "hot rod"...his first car.

The Edsel (supposedly) was "revolutionary." It was due to be unveiled in late September, 1957. Nearby was University Ford. Being on Belmont, it was close to our house. I kept thinking...Edsel? What a dumb name for a car. To me, it sounded more like some new dance - introduced by Dick Clark on "American Bandstand."

"HEY, c'mon EVERYONE..."Let's do the EDSEL!"

And so - being a curious, car-loving little kid- I began pedaling my Schwinn bike up to University Ford in late September. On the crowded showroom floor, were two large cars covered COMPLETELY with brown canvas. Then, September 29...at last! The mysterious covers would come off. The official revealing of the all-new Edsel. September 29: It was around 7PM - Dad and I pulled into the Ford dealer's parking lot: it was almost empty.

Dad and I wondered..."Where is everyone?" As soon as Dad and I saw the two Edsels inside, we came to an abrupt "halt." Unbelievable: both Edsels were appallingly-ugly – looking rather distorted.

One car was a bizzare turquoise color...the other was a strange "off pink"...like the color of the eraser in my pencil box.

The Edsel's protruding front grille gave the car the appearance of a battering ram. It was actually hideous! The side profile was hideous. The tail lights were obscenely HIDEOUS.

Could Ford not have seen what they'd done- then do a redesign? Dad was shaking his head:..."Let's go home." Driving back home, Dad - utterly disappointed - was silent.

I wondered: How could Ford make a car look so incredibly UGLY? Had they done it on PURPOSE? Sure seemed that way. Back to the present: Sept 27, 1965: Dwight and I walked into Valley Pontiac: It was like "Deja Vu" when I first saw an EDSEL: "Holy baloney! WHAT is this thing?" We were taken aback.

The weird-looking 66 GTO had been totally distorted! – looking completely different from the sleek 65 GTO. The car was grossly oversized...sort of pudgy-wudgy look - deserving of being called a "pig." The streamlined, sleek, 1965 GTO was gone. The

66 GTO had asymmetrical curves running everywhere. I was AGHAST! The 65 GTO tiger had been transmuted into a barnyard, 66 wart hog. Dwight seemed bewildered- right hand on his chin, as he kept encircling the car: "Hmmm; what is THIS?"

I thought it cluttered...peculiar-looking. There was no "styling theme" (i.e.) throw a lot of spaghetti and see what sticks to the wall. To me, it was like waking-up...INTO A NIGHTMARE.

The elongated roof line was all rounded curves. I wondered... Why would they alter the gorgeous angular roofline of the 65 GTO? The curving front grille looked downright weird. The enclosed parking lamps - within the grille - only added more clutter; as if some Pontiac engineer had decided to throw additional spaghetti!

The 66 GTO was pure Fat City. No more "little GTO." A heavier car is a SLOWER car. I thought..."Damm, this '66 porker must be 2 tons."

To me, the over-sized, hooded, horizontal tail lights looked overstated and out of proportion. The back quarter panels ended in a bizarre, geometric shape at the rear bumper. I absolutely despised this horrendous, hoggy-looking 1966 GTO! Lord have mercy!

Then, raising the hood - another shock: Pontiac had even changed the engine block color - from a robust, royal blue; to a wimpy-looking, blue-green metallic.

But WHY? Dwight - using his index finger - had traced "GRRRR" in the thick dust on top of the flat, "pancake" air cleaner; about the only feature carried over from 65 GTO. But 66 GTOs did not growl. They would prove to be toothless tigers. Lazy dogs - running as if they carried cement blocks in their trunks. I could scarcely believe my eyes! No-ooo! Worst of all: Pontiac- in their infinite wisdom- foolishly ALTERED their iconic '65 389 engine - proving disastrous.

What the devil were they thinking? Valve diameters. Engine ports, camshaft and ignition timing - all mindlessly changed. By December '65, the word was out on the street... "66 GTOs do NOT run...THEY'RE PIGS!"

As the saying goes..."If it ain't broke, DON'T fix it." So doggy were the 66 389 engines, that an "all-new" 400 cubic inch motor was introduced for 1967.

Disconsolate, I wondered..."Why would Pontiac attempt to modify PERFECTION?" It was like forcing Marilyn Monroe to undergo plastic surgery: Or transforming Elvis into a ballet dancer; or refurbishing the beautiful, classic spire of the Chrysler building, in New York. Walking home, I was actually near tears.

It was like one of those old, World War 2 drama movies; where the opening scene depicts Mom 'n Dad at the train station - bidding farewell to their handsome soldier son - going off to war overseas.

Then, 2 years later, the son steps off the train – horribly disfigured - from a grievous wound from the war. The parents recoil in horror! - barely able to look at their unfortunate son; whose life has been shattered. Yes. I'm going a bit overboard here. But that was exactly how I felt when I first saw that damm, hoggish '66 GTO! A complete DISASTER! I kept mumbling to myself..."They completely ruined it...Why would they ruin perfection?"

Chapter 9

OCTOBER: 1965

Thursday afternoon - I had just arrived home after school: Mom said, "Mona just called; she wants you to call her back." I dialed...thinking..."probably needs her GTO washed."

Mona: "Hello Rick? Can you come out tomorrow afternoon, and pick up the GTO? It needs washed & waxed...and the interior needs cleaned."

"Sure Mona, what's up?"

"Saturday night, I'm taking some new pledges to our sorority exchange dinner. Keep the GTO Friday night and bring it back Saturday morning; and I'll take you home."

WOW! I was on cloud NINE- thinking about driving her stunning, lipstick-red GTO...on a FRIDAY night!

Indeed, Mona - wanting to impress her sorority sisters - knew I'd have her goat looking showroom new.

No one could clean a car like ME. And man, how I loved doing it. All Thursday night, I could barely fall asleep - kept thinking about Mona's rocket-fast GTO - making the BIG impression on everyone who might see me.

Mona HATED washing her car: Maybe an occasional trip to the auto wash; but seldom more. So I was - literally - "Johnnie on the spot."

Time check: Friday 5 PM. Like two eager beavers, Frank and I got REALLY busy on Mona's grimy goat. Frank worked on the bumpers - shining the chrome like new.

After washing & polishing it to a spectacular, beaming high gloss, I carefully vacuumed the interior. The tiniest speck of debris had vanished. Even the dusty, inside of the back window got a streak-free cleaning.

Friday 8 pm: Frankie and I headed out Market Street. It seemed a DREAM: A spotless, gleaming-like-new 65 GTO; and ME behind the wheel!

We drove all the way out to Route 224 in Boardman - cruising through "Morgan's Big Boy" (i.e.) the big south side drive-in. But this wasn't your typical, 60's "burger joint."

Morgan's was HUGE!

Everyone went there - a place just like a movie: waitresses zipping along the long rows of cars - carrying chrome trays - to feed the "hungry masses."

But food was secondary. Showing off one's car in the parking lot was the PRIMARY attraction:

There were "bad-boys" cruising around - heads postured arrogantly...driving 327 4-speed Chevies. Mustangs galore. A black '64 Corvette. Chevy Malibus. Cutlass Oldsmobiles...but hardly any GTOs.

Frank and I were like, "Wow" when we pulled in. Everyone "froze"... and was pointing at us - driving among the long rows of cars. Mona's GTO was Cinderella amongst a parking lot of her "stepsisters" - easily the SHARPEST car on the entire lot!

The place was huge - drawfing Red Barn - jammed with over ONE HUNDRED cars. Mona's stunning GTO shined like a bright star on the horizon.

A 62 Impala - six chicks aboard - were pointing at Mona's sleek, 65 GTO: completely awestruck. I could read their lips: "WOW...look at that red GTO!"

Instantly, I began following them - wanting to get friendly with THAT car full of young ladies. But Frank wanted to race: He could be a real pain in the glutes- insisting that we go back onto Market Street and blow away anyone next to us at a red light.

Reluctantly, I pulled back onto Market- heading toward Youngstown. Nevertheless, I was in no mood to take chances. An accident or ticket would be ruinous. Also possible damage to the GTO's engine or transmission.

I recalled how Johnnie Marino had so RECKLESSLY torn up his GTO... in no time at all.

Besides, it was a riot showing off! Getting thumbs up. People waving. Pointing. Blasting the radio. Playing king of the road!

Let everyone think this stunning GTO belonged to ME. Who knew otherwise? I was enjoying ALL the attention- driving a 65 GTO! My celestial DREAM car!

I wanted to savor the moment. The smooth "feel"of the road: "G-r-r-r-r-r-r"... how this GTO sounded. The whole overall car - just PERFECT.

Ironically: it was the ONE time in my entire life that I was NOT keyed-up for a street race.

But Market Street on a Friday night was a "destination spot" (i.e.) an allurement for ANY hot shot; out to prove that he - and his car - were the "baddest" anywhere around.

In the 1960s, one's ego was largely defined by the car you drove. You and your car – psychologically - became one and the same.

Sure enough - nearing the Youngstown border - a red 65 Dodge 383 Coronet pulls alongside: Yet another arrogant Mopar driver..."with something to prove."

He was cocky...self-assured - looking over at us disdainfully. I kept looking at the "Commando V8" badge displayed on his front fender.

The light ahead turned red: I looked over at the red Coronet: guy driving was a typical Mopar cretin – acting like he's some ruff-tuff cream puff, in his big-bad 383 Coronet.

These same Mopar drivers would be cruising through Red Barn - each acting like they were some total bad-azz. Same with this dolt beside me.

The light changed! The Dodge streaked away! While I carefully pulled out nice 'n SLOW; like a student in driver training.... No drag-racing ticket for ME.

Frank voiced his disapproval: "What the F**K ARE YOU DOING? - you CHICKEN sh*t!"

Frank was not real pleased that I had "dogged out" of racing the Dodge. But I had a ready "alibi."

"Thought I saw a police cruiser three cars back. I'm not gonna risk a ticket by some Boardman cop. In Youngstown, I would've blown his doors off."

Good answer. A traffic ticket in Youngstown could easily be 'fixed." The night passed without further incident...until 11 PM:

A dazzling, shining, gorgeous black 65 GTO (4-speed) pulls alongside us at a redlight. Guy driving seemed cool...cocky... laid back...confident. His new, black 65 GTO was so unbelievingly beautiful.

Reading his aloof facial expression, I knew he was running three deuce carbs (tri-power) underneath the hood. Thinking fast, window down, I yelled..."Lets go to Lockwood, and race from a tromp."

The glistening, black GTO followed us to nearby Lockwood Boulevard: It was wide. Smooth. Two miles long... and NO cops. Perfect for street-racing.

It looked deserted. I kept thinking of the surprise that awaited this cocky guy in his TRIPOWER goat: From a rolling start (tromp) Mona's 4 barrel GTO was incredibly-FAST: When you punched the gas, it was like poking a gigantic hornet's nest! "RRRRRRRRRRRRRR".

Window rolled down, I yelled..."we'll go on three." As we rolled alongside each other, I remember this driver (about 23 - clean-cut) was trying NOT to laugh. Man, was he ever in for an eye-opener!

I gave the command: "Go on three: One...two...THREE!"

I mashed the gas pedal: "SCREEECH" - incredibly, Mona's GTO jumped up like a WILD HORSE - laying down a long strip - and we went STORMING away to an amazing 3 car lead!

In my mirror, this driver looked totally dismayed...almost in panic mode. Frank and I were in stitches! - trying to imagine what this ASTONISHED driver was thinking: "J-E-E-E-ZUSS KEE-REIST! What the hell's in that goat?"

This driver was smiling no longer. He had that "Oh Sh*t I'm behind" look on his face. But with tripower carbs- I knew what was coming:

In the left lane behind me, I saw his headlights jerk-upwardly as hit 4th gear. The noise was UNREAL...."GARR-ROOOOOOOOOOOM"

Frank was losing it..."Here he comes!"

After pulling even, he 'eased away' to an 1/2 car lead. We were at 100 mph when I backed off the gas.

WOW...so electrifying! "The Friday night shoot out on Lockwood Blvd." It was indeed high-voltage excitement! Something I would never forget.

After coming oh-so-close to whipping a mighty TRIPOWER 65 GTO, I felt so damm proud - driving Mona's GTO. No sore loser was I that night.

AFTERMATH: This guy was cool - not crowing in victory. Judging by the look on his face - he was duly impressed! - kind of "diplomatic" even.

He rolled down his window..."WOW! That's a pretty good running automatic...is that tri-power?" Holding up four fingers (four barrel) I yelled back..."Your goat's a tri-power...Right?"

Nodding "yes" he zipped away. Time-check: 11:45 PM. We decided to head for Belmont Ave - to get to the Red Barn. The night was still young.

Chapter 10

APRIL: 1966

Word was spreading all over the street: 66 GTOs were pitiful hogs - running like lethargic dogs.

One night, I was hanging out at Isaly's. Along comes Tommy "Gibbie" Gibson - PROUDLY showing off his new, white 66 GTO.

He lived nearby. Immediately the hood was opened; and everyone saw the impressive, iconic, Pontiac triple 2 barrel carb arrangement (i.e.) TRI-POWER

This 66 GTO - sporting 3 deuces - looked REALLY kick-azz. Gibbie was actually walking with a swagger...he was driving a TRIPOWER GTO!

I thought..."what a joke."

On Market Street I'd seen - WITH MY OWN EYES - 66 GTOs getting stir-fried by SS 396 Chevelles: a HUGE embarrassment to all Pontiac lovers (like me).

Just then, one of Gibbie's buddies opened the passenger door. Riding shotgun, the two were off for a "test" ride.

But this GTO would flunk...big time.

Gibbie was literally "beaming" with pride. Everyone watching. His GTO started with a fearsome "WHOOOM." The dual exhausts rumbling LOUDLY.

Gibbie - after rolling 30 feet - punched the gas.

"GR-OOOOOOOOM."

His tripower carbs sounded awesome. But his taillights did not "disappear down the street." From my viewing perspective, I could see his 66 GOAT wasn't really fast at all.

It was all sound; but NO FURY. Indeed, all around Youngstown, SS 396 Chevelles were blowing away 66 GTOs - like a hurricane howling through a trailer park. And what about Pontiac?

Most certainly they knew that 66 GTOs were losing badly on the street. But it seemed as though they could care less.

In 1965, 75,000 GTOs were sold. But in 66, over 100,000. A 25% increase. GTOs were now being sold on their IMAGE - rather than a tire-scorching, street-fightin' machine.

Was Pontiac's formidable GTO; once a ferocious tiger - now on the verge of BECOMING extinct? It was all so unbelievably perplexing: Why did Pontiac - once the CLEAR leader in street performance - choose to wimp out vs. the competition? (i.e.) the SS 396 Chevelle...Oldsmobile's 66 442; and Chrysler's newly-introduced streethemi. Since the late 50s, Pontiac had always been a step ahead of the competition – always upgrading the overall performance of every model.

A '66 Oldsmobile 442

Ergo, If you drove a Pontiac, you KNEW that you were getting the MOST CAR for your money vs. any other brand of automobile. FLASHBACK - summer 1959 - I was 10: My brother and I were playing "catch" in front of our house. It was Friday around 7 pm. Then, this HUGE new car parks right in front of us. It was bright red, 59 Pontiac Bonneville CONVERTIBLE; with a white top - driven by Lou Marinelli, Dad's best bricklayer.... stopping by for his weekly paycheck.

I was stunned! I put down my glove - THOROUGHLY astonished. This 59 Bonneville was truly a car 'for the ages." One of the most beautiful cars I'd ever seen!

I looked at the front end and grille. Such ornate chrome! Walking around the entire car, I could not believe the tailfins. The taillights...the side ornamentation...the interior. It was all so incredibly beautiful: Pontiac had outdone themselves.

(3 years later)

By summer 1962, our 56 Ford Sunliner convertible had "rusted out."

Mom 'n Dad could've afforded any mid-priced car. Final pick? A gorgeous 1962 Pontiac Bonneville - burgundy with WHITE interior. Said Mom..."One of the most beautiful cars I've ever seen."

Dad was thrilled: the Bonneville came standard with a big 389 cubic inch motor with a FOUR barrel carb.

In 1959, Pontiac introduced tri-power: triple two barrel carbs (i.e.) three deuces. Put the pedal to the metal and hear that unbelievable tri-power GROWL: Driving a tri-power Pontiac, you could "clean house" at red lights. Such a pleasure; so satisfying! You felt as if you were KING of the road! Oh yeah!

FLASHBACK: June 1963: a seminal event: the unofficial birth of the Pontiac GTO; which literally changed the world!

John DeLorean - Pontiac's brilliant head engineer - was drawing a sketch on a restaurant napkin during lunch.

It was "WHAT IF" time: "What if you took a 389 cubic inch motor (full sized Pontiac) and dropped it into a LeMans? (mid size car). What then?"

The idea quickly caught fire: A mock-up 64 LeMans was hoisted up, and the standard 326 cubic inch V8 was swapped-out for Pontiac's iconic 389 cubic inch engine.

The result would change history.

The new prototype car - named "GTO" - was so much fun to drive, that when DeLorean loaned out the car, he'd have a helluva time trying to get it returned.

For model year 1964, the buzz about the amazingly-fast GTO was so overwhelming, that Pontiac dealers (nationwide) ordered 5000 GTOs in advance - having no idea all about the CAR they would actually be getting.

A 1981 Delorean Automobile

"Fortune favors the BOLD."

NOTE: in the early 1980s - in Ireland- after John DeLorean began manufacturing his DeLorean automobile there; sales of the STAINLESS STEEL sports car began to "sizzle."

But within the year, the DeLorean sizzle had become the "great FIZZLE." Overall, owners loved the car; but despised its pitiful V-6-cylinder engine- cranking out a pathetic 130 HORSEPOWER - hardly exceeding that of a Vespa motor scooter.

Now imagine this: it's 1981; and you're living in Pasadena; and your new DeLorean car arrives from overseas.

Then on your first Sunday drive, you're next to the "little old lady from Pasadena"- driving to church - in her Buick Park Avenue:

Light changes....and "r-r-r-r-r-r"...the little old lady has blown you COMPLETELY away! Your piddling DeLorean couldn't even come CLOSE; with its pipsqueak, 130 horsepower V-6: enough to beat a rickshaw - or the Oscar Meyer Weinermobile; but not much else.

Now, let's imagine ALL the other DeLorean owners during the 1980's: The DeLorean cars were super-sleek; built low to the ground; like a FERRARI. Ergo, the DeLorean cars LOOKED super fast! But then, the inevitable: some hot shot - in a Datsun 280 ZX - pulls up beside YOU at a red light- ready to race your DeLorean; a race you CANNOT even fathom to win.

Even worse: your new GIRL FRIEND is riding along beside you. Go ahead man. ENJOY that big slice of humble pie. Hard to swallow, eh? Next, you're going up a steep hill; and then, some VW bug scoots right past you – like YOU'RE STANDING STILL! Subconsciously, you're thinking..."Gawd, how I hate this pizz-poor, SLOW piece of sh*t." Not surprisingly, DeLorean automobiles ceased all production in 1982 - going belly-up (bankrupt) - after just 2 years. It was all so ironic: John DeLorean- father of the super-fast 64 GTO- had made a colossal blunder! If he'd put a small block V8 under the hood, the Delorean car would still be selling today. Americans EXPECTED speed in a sports car; and the DeLorean car had everything imaginable...but SPEED.

Zero-to-sixty, a tripower 64 GTO had been clocked in 4.6 seconds! WOW. Never had any other mass-production car even come CLOSE to such an incredible time. 64 GTO owners would now experience "racial inequality."

In a street RACE, nothing could EQUAL the sheer acceleration of the 64 GTO! Take on a GTO and see tail lights rapidly disappearing down the highway...the driver gleefully waving "BYE BYE."

In 1965, Pontiac - always the leader - introduced their iconic 65 GTO; but they'd made it even FASTER!

The all new 65 GTO had state-of-art improvements: D-shaped engine ports. 10:75 to 1 compression. Higher lift, longer-duration McKellar camshaft. Transistorized ignition. 421 Super Duty engine heads. 65 GTO owners were now singing the new Dave Clark Five hit..."Catch Us if You Can." Driving a 65 GTO was like a Toyota commercial: "Oh what a feeling."

But then came model year 1966. Pontiac - always improving - had gone TOO far. Nearly every aspect of the legendary 65 389 motor was modified; an unmitigated disaster! Camshaft. Engine heads. Valve diameters. Ignition timing. etc...all changed for the worse.

The all new 66 GTOs were just plain SLOW!

"Slower than an ice wagon"...one of my Dad's favorite expressions. How about "slower than molasses?"

BOTTOM LINE: Most Americans despise almost anything slow: particularly their cars.

Throughout American history, it was all about "GOING FASTER!"

In the early 19th century, Fulton invented the steam ship. Now, a steam powered vessel could navigate much FASTER, going up-river, against a swift, downriver current.

In the early 19th century, the steam locomotive came to the forefront. At 20 miles per hour, it was considered stunningly FAST, vs. any other mode of transportation.

In the 1840's, Morse code allowed information to travel FASTER...in actual REAL time; vs a horse-mounted messenger carrier.

Then, a FASTER way to get mail to the far West (i.e.) the legendary Pony Express May 1869: the completion of the Transcontinental Railroad, allowed travelers to cross the American continent MUCH FASTER: in FIVE DAYS; rather than three months in a wagon train.

Of course, we all know the story of Henry Ford; and his model T - linking rural America with urban America. Now one could travel inter-city much FASTER!

Then came the V8 engine - enabling cars to go much FASTER! Think about it: Did not America become the greatest nation on earth, because Americans did everything FASTER? Our American dialect gives testimony to the importance of doing everything FAST. "GET YOUR REAR IN GEAR"...HURRY UP...GET GOING...DOUBLE TIME...C'MON, SLOW POKE..GET MOVING...GET THE LEAD OUT....LET'S ROLL...GOD SPEED...FULL SPEED AHEAD...C'mon, STEP ON IT."

Consider: has anyone EVER - other a traffic cop - told you to "slow down?" Has there ever been a TV commercial..."Come to beautiful Cedar Point, and ride the world's SLOWEST roller coaster."

Absurd! How about triple crown race tracks? Do not people flock there to see the FASTEST thoroughbreds in America? Golf tournaments...the PGA: considered by many as TOO SLOW to watch on TV.

Major League baseball - now considered a "slowly-dying game"... vs. ever-rising NFL television viewership; because NFL football is much FASTER.

The American workplace: has there ever been an employee terminated for WORKING TOO FAST? Move too slow and "you've got to GO!" (i.e.) "Don't let the screen door hit you in the azz!"

Recall Peter Paul & Mary's 1969 hit song - "I'm Leaving on a Jet Plane." Now compare that to..."I'm Leaving on a Propeller Plane."

Again absurd!

How about the term "speed demon?" Has anyone ever been called a "SLOW DEMON?"

In baseball, a player who easily steals bases, is often called a "SPEED MERCHANT."

Conversely, should not a slow-afoot player be known as a "SLOW MERCHANT?"

In major league baseball, slow players have little chance - unless they're CATCHERS.

Fans will not tolerate some "ice wagon" lumbering around the bases; let alone playing outfield.

Referring back to propeller planes; we cannot forget the fantastic World War Two P-51 Mustang; the US fighter plane that literally WON the European theater of the war.

A P-51 Mustang- World War 2 Fighter Plane

From fall 1943, to early 1945, the Allies fought hard to achieve air superiority; but still lacked complete CONTROL of the skies.

Then, in fall, 1944, squadrons of the amazing Mustangs arrived in large numbers - making an immediate and CRITICAL difference.

The P-51 had superior range - could fly deep into Germany, and return. The Mustang could out-climb, out-turn, out-dive, ANY German plane; an incredible DOG FIGHTER!

And most important of all, the Mustang had a sizzling 447 MPH top speed; a full 50 MPH advantage over any front-line German fighter.

When US B-17 bomber crews first spotted the Mustangs alongside - flying in escort - they LITERALLY had tears of JOY running down their cheeks! Now they'd have a chance to return ALIVE! Casualty rates for B-17 crews were appalling - approaching 75% at that time. Actually, what they experienced was HELL

ABOVE the earth. Easily spotted by German radar, flights of the nightmarish Focke Wulf 190 fighters were directed to within a few miles of the American bomber formations: and so would begin a horrible bloody slaughter:

Flying just beyond range of the B-17s fifty calibers; a wing of Focke Wulfs would - one by one - fly down firing at the tail gunner; until he was dead. Then, the all-but-helpless B-17s were literally SITTING DUCKS - unprotected from the rear against the ever-lethal 20 millimeter cannons of the FW 190.

When a brave young tailgunner - who managed to shoot down a FW 190 - was asked by American press reporters how he'd done it, he replied..."I gave him the whole NINE yards." (i.e.) B-17 fifty caliber ammo belts measured out to nine yards in length.

The tables were quickly turned: No longer were the Nazi Luftwaffe (air force) fighters able to get anywhere near the US bomber squadrons - flying en masse over Berlin.

The Mustangs would be on them like chocolate on a klondike - blasting them into FRAGMENTS; with their awesome array of firepower...SIX Browning fifty caliber machine guns; three in each wing.

WOW...that's a whole lotta lead!

There is an anecdotal story about a quote from German Air Marshall, Herman Goering...QUOTE:

"If Germany had the Browning.50 caliber, ve vould have WON the war."

Another anecdotal story about Goering: Reportedly, the slim 'n trim Marshall Goering - about 150 lbs. (give or take) overweight - was having his three hour breakfast, in his hilltop mansion, outside Berlin: then he heard a thundering of engines: He drew back the window curtains: QUOTE:

"Harrumph. Mustangs over Berlin. Those gotverdammrung Amerikaners! Now ve have lost the war for sure....more schnitzel please!"

Well of course the Americans went on to finish the war - largely due to their obsession for speed!

And they all lived happily ever AFTER!

Chapter 11

MAY 1966:

It was my last month of school: A time of light-heartedness...rejoicing...merry-making! And of course - havin' a BLAST, going to class.

It was the final countdown...I was about to graduate from high school! (play Alice Cooper"School's Out")

But big trouble was in the air: BIG trouble for yours truly (me). WHY? I was always bragging incessantly about Pontiac GTOs!

(perhaps too much).

And why not?

A growling, howling, thundering GTO would blow you RIGHT off the street! Pontiac's prodigious tri-power GTO was a "world beater. "Just punch that throttle and WHOOOM - it was like a volcano erupting under your hood!"

"Look out BELOW!"

GTOs were such fun cars! UNBELIEVABLY FAST! Such neck-snapping acceleration! WAROOOOOOM! What an unbelievable sound...GRRRRRRRRRRRRRR.

YEAH: A Pontiac GTO - amazingly quick from a red light! - especially when some kornhole pulls up beside you- driving his 327 SS Chevy. He hasn't GOT a chance:

"GRROOOOOOOOOOM."

"Bye-bye, Mr. 327 CHEVY! Be safe. Have a blessed day...shalom!" etc. From 63 to 66, NOTHING on the street could run with a sizzling-hot 389 GTO tiger!

I But then the inevitable downfall: it would happen on September 27, 1965: As Don McClain might say: "The day the tiger died..."

Let me explain to y'all. Sept. 27, 1965: It was the day when the ALL-NEW 66 GTO was revealed. The whole automotive world had been waiting...especially me.

As it turned out, the all-new, weird-looking 66 GTOs were the Edsels of the mid-1960s. (fat & oversized) The hideous 58 Edsel, along with the hoggish 66 GTO, saw many potential new car customers - hitting "reverse" upon first sight.

In model year 1966 - for some inexplicable reason - Pontiac engineers had sat on their collective rear-ends: No GTO performance upgrades were forthcoming. Nothing new at all.

The new 66 GTOs WERE total laggards on the street: and now, to my great dismay - they were dubbed as "PIGS!"

All around town, 66 GTOs were running as if they were pulling a loaded U-HAUL. Unlike a TIGER 65 GTO; the 66 goat was all-pork...a USDA-certified hog.

SEPTEMBER- 1965:

Sensing an opportunity to take market share vs. Pontiac - eager competitors now began "leap-frogging" ahead: The 66 Olds 442 (one of the hottest cars ever) featured a higher-compression, higher-horsepower 400 motor: Optional were tripower carbs, radio delete...trunk-mounted battery – spelling big trouble for ANYONE who raced them.

In the 1966 NHRA nationals, a 66 442 ("B" stock) - sponsored by Chesrown Olds in Columbus - won with the ASTONISHING time of 12.97 for the 1/4 mile...not too shabby.

Chevy- not to take a back seat - introduced their classic SS Chevelle; which came standard with a nasty, high-torque 396 "rat" motor. Yet another "Goat Eater."

Chrysler now introduced its MONSTER, dual-quad 425 hp street hemi; available on Plymouth Belvedere; or Dodge Coronet. Oldsmobile then introduced its W-30 engine option- built strictly for street racing. These cars were screamers...establishing the 442 W-30 as one of the baddest, fastest cars of all time. Decimating from ANY red light.

Meanwhile, farty old Pontiac continued doing NOTHING; just sat around apathetically- watching once-loyal patrons rejecting mediocrity: customers that would NEVER return. I remembered when "it all began."

FLASHBACK: October 1965. Arby's had opened on Belmont...the hot new hangout; the place to be SEEN. The place to GO.

One November Friday night, Arby's was mobbed after our high school won its championship game. Then came a show-stopper: It was Lenny Cervone - a "west sider" - driving his shiny-new, pacific-blue, 66 SS 396 Chevelle, 325 horsepower 4-speed.

Wow; was it ever a beauty WHITE INTERIOR; a so-cool "knee-knocker" tach below the dashboard! Factory "spinner" mag wheels. A drop-dead gorgeous car!

When Cervone first drove into Arby's parking lot, his SS Chevelle was surrounded immediately - like a movie star walking down Sunset Strip Boulevard.

And then, Tommy O'Donnell's red, 66 tripower GTO pulls into Arbys; and the big SHOWDOWN was ON! Immediately, both the Chevelle and GTO were headed WAY out to Belmont Ave "extension" - for a run-off (no cops to look out for) Curses! I was trapped (back seat) in some nurd's crappy 62 Corvair. (forgot his name) Anyway, nurd-man "had to have the car home by

ELEVEN." So I didn't get to see the big race; but next Monday, I would most certainly find out:

Monday, 2nd period lunch: in the cafeteria kitchen: I'm pushing my tray along the three metal rails...when "bang." Looking to my left, it was Tommy Zarlenga; who loved Chevrolets; who'd crashed into my tray.

He mumbled something ominous under his breath..."Tell me all about your GTOs, Sandine!" Such hostility! I was puzzled.

Then - sitting down to eat lunch- a "parade" of Chevy lovers began harassing me at my table: "Ha-hah Sandine! How do like you GTOs now? They're all PIGS!"

Later, in the men's room - at the adjacent urinal - was Joe Hudzik- laughing scornfully..."Hah hah Sandine; how's them hoggy goats runnin'? They're ALL PIGS. "Ha ha. Ho ho. Yuk-yuk" etc.

Almost immediately thereafter, I proceeded to my 5th period English class:

My gawd; I'd just sat down at my desk; when this white trash punk, William Jones, whispers across the aisle..."Hey Sandine. Didja hear about O'Donnell's goat? Hah hah! Dem goats are all pigs...ho-ho...hee-hee."

Instantly, I realized I was a 'marked man.' Like some police manhunt - wary of anywhere I might go! Turns out that Cervone's Chevelle had "blown the doors off" O'Donnell's 66 tripower goat, by six cars!(6 car lengths) I became completely dismayed! Even paranoid! When the 2:55 pm dismissal bell rang, it was time to "get outta Dodge!" I literally bolted out the exit door – looking over my shoulder.

I felt like David Janssen from the TV series..."The Fugitive." But that was only the beginning: All around town, 66 GTOs were getting slaughtered; like freshly-plucked chickens in a butcher shop.

But somehow, the blame had been ascribed to ME. Finally it dawned upon stupid-dumbell me. My constant bragging about the "unbeatable" GTO had created bitter antipathy. Now, sore-loser Chevy men claimed their revenge.

Previously, Chevy 409s and 327 Chevys just couldn't compete on the street vs. the blistering-fast 64-65 GTOs.

Now, SS 396 Chevelles were the new monsters of Market street- showing no mercy on the hapless, hopeless 66 goats.

For me it became a living nightmare: the ridicule was cruel & unending; especially at LUNCHTIME. Eat in the cafeteria? No way. Hide in the gym? Nope. Basketball practice.

Going outside? Instantly I'd be cornered by Chevy men..."Ha ha Sandine. ALL GOATS are PIGS." It was like Alcatraz; there was no escaping it! I began to think of that hit Motown song, by Martha 'n the Vandellas..."No Where to Run, Nowhere to Hide."

My Lord! How I made it through those last months of my senior year, I'll never know. Finally June 4, 1966: Graduation day! I felt like Martin Luther King - giving his 1963 speech: "FREE AT LAST!"

The happiest day of my entire life!

I would - most likely - NEVER see any of those Chevrolet cretins again.

(two weeks later)

It was the second Sunday in June: Frankie Malone came up with a dynamite IDEA...check out Skyline dragstrip (New Castle PA) and witness the GTO slaughter firsthand. Skyline was only 30 minutes away; about 15 miles southeast of Youngstown.

Skyline dragstrip was so cool! They were strict about who could compete. If you registered "stock," then pure factory stock it was. No racing slicks. Factory stock tires only.

No horrible "Gasser" cars. No insipid rail dragsters; with those insanely large back tires! No ugly hot rods - with their deafening open exhaust pipes!

No modifications whatsoever. Even better: they had a flagman; which meant you could NOT anticipate your opponent - vs. an NHRA "christmas tree" electronic starter. Upon entering, we paid for a pit pass, so we'd get an upfront look at all cars competing that day.

There were no less than twenty five, 66 442s in the vast pit area: and indeed - they were dishing out a serious beat-down on all the SS Chevelles; plus the hoggy-doggy 66 goats.

Unbelievable - in the time trials every 66 442 won its race. Predictably, every 66 GTO got demolished...some by 5,6, even 7 car lengths. Wow. It was astonishing - watching a 442 pull away- zooming down the asphalt 1/4 mile track; with hapless 66 GTO, trailing WAY behind. Frank and I just stood there watching in shock - reluctant to admit that indeed, ALL 66 goats were PIGS. It was now 4 PM: time for the big "runoff." Said the announcer..."All SUPER STOCK cars registered, please come to the starting line."

At once, a gold 66 Plymouth Belvedere emerges; with "Strictly Street Hemi" painted on each door. (cool name) Then appears a burgundy 66 427 Chevy Biscayne; with its splendid "427 Turbo-Jet badges" on each front fender.

Both cars - poised aside the flagman - were racing their engines...spinning their rear tires- creating clouds of blue/grey tire smoke.

SUSPENSE: everyone anticipating the HEMI would win: but who knew?

The crowd was HUSHED. Even the wise-cracking announcer seemed at a loss for words. 427 Biscayne? Few had ever seen or heard of one...including me. The flagman signaled "ready" to both drivers: When the flag wet down, it was shocking: The Biscayne came roaring out of the hole like a thunderbolt of lightning! - with a deafening, screaming "E-E-E-E-E-E-ROOOOOM."

This car was the fastest thing I'd ever seen! The high winding 427 rat motor - hitting 7000 RPM! The Biscayne driver hit 4th gear. Unbelievable - he was at least 10 car lengths ahead of the Plymouth hemi...unreal!

"Strictly Street Hemi" was a sheep in wolf's clothing...a pitiful dog! - running as if it were hauling anthracite coal in its trunk.

A spectator behind us was heard: "WOW, that 427 beat that hemi by half the track!"

Thoroughly humiliated, never again was "Strictly Street Hemi" to be seen at Skyline drag strip.

Later, on the way home - it was appalling! I could not stop thinking about how quickly the "pig" 66 GTO had COMPLETELY demolished the Pontiac GTO's reputation - forever. No longer would the GTO ever again be called a "tiger." But it was fun while it lasted...

Chapter 12

A '64 GTO Convertible

SEPTEMBER 1966

Moving into a dormitory, I commenced my freshman year at OSU. My dream- Ohio State! I couldn't wait!

I expected a vibrant, pulsating campus- lovely COEDS...raucous PARTIES everywhere!

Nope. Quite the opposite...a big "fizzle." Columbus was largely inhabited by docile,"country folks" (i.e.) hillbillies.

During World War 2, West Virginians migrated to Columbus en masse - working in munitions factories. They were crucial in America's hugely successful domestic war effort.

After the war, the hilljacks stayed - blending into the cultural "melting pot." They lived everywhere - particularly on the city's sprawling west side.

They had a discernible accent - Ohio State became... "OHIA" state. It was culture shock!

Columbus cops were totally anal. The first time I went to cross N. High street, a motorcycle cop swooped over and yelled..."You can't cross here! Use the painted crosswalk!"I feared he'd write a jaywalking ticket!

He was mean! Instantly I began to HATE Columbus! Their cops were revenuers. Bloodsuckers. "City of Columbus" tow trucks prowling everywhere - impounding cars. Unreal!

Even worse: Columbus had NO ethnic people. No Italians. No Italian bread in stores! I felt lost!

Worst of all: "Muscle" cars were practically NON existent on North High St. - the main thoroughfare bordering the campus. It was "cold turkey"...No Corvettes. Few GTOs - even fewer SS Chevelles. But lots of "compact" motorcycles - mostly Hondas...going "putt-putt" down the street.

A 1966 Honda Motorcycle

I felt like I'd landed on Mars! There was no Belmont. No *MARKET street*: Nowhere to street race! No place to go cruising; or hang out.

Homesick, I depended on letters from Youngstown as a "survival mechanism."

My dormitory? it was the WORST! A bunch of rural, Ohio-born bumpkins- sitting in their dorm rooms like old retirees- playing "gin rummy." They were no FUN at all.

They all seemed quite content to play this insipid, inane card game. Nevertheless, I remained the only "outlier" on my floor. I didn't feel like associating with any of them.

And the dorm "food?" Shiny roast beef - served with "taste free" starchy mashed potatoes. Day old bread. Horrible-looking, horrible tasting watery "chocolate" pudding, for so-called "desert."

For a place serving food, it smelled terrible; like something was burning. Fortunately - as an alternative - there was a peanut butter cart with various flavors of jelly. Otherwise, I would've starved to death.

My dorm roommate, "Murph" (Jim Murphy) was an "OK" guy - from Oneida county in upstate New York. Murph had a curious verbal idiosyncracy - "douche bag." Obviously a derogatory term. He would use it as a noun, adjective, pronoun...(e.g.) "Those guys from Toledo across the hall are douche bags."...or..."Some douche bag in my English class tried to sell me a tape recorder."

Murph also insisted I play "gin" with him. The stupidest card game EVER.

I remembered when I was 8 years old; how my Aunt Phyllis had taught me "GO FISH." To me, matching suits in "gin" differed little from "GO FISH."

At least poker required strategy; plus the suspense. How 'bout a card game of WAR?

Murph and I had one thing in common...we loved the Buckeyes! OSU football was king.

Day before classes, we both picked up our "student activity" books – containing 5 home game tickets. You could attend football games as part of the "student body."

Next Saturday, we went to see the home opener: the Buckeyes vs. the Oregon "Ducks."

All excited! We thought we'd be sitting in the center of the action with all the other red-clad OSU students on the 40 yard line.

Nope. We found our "temporary seating area"- flimsy collapsible folding chairs- set up on the cinder running track...at "field level" near the goal line. We had a great view of the flagpole in the north end zone.

The absolute WORST seats in Ohio Stadium! Plus, we'd come WAY too early - at least 45 minutes before kick-off. Then it started raining. Within minutes we were soaked. Then - at kickoff - two *miracles* occurred: The sun came out. And RIGHT before our eyes...twelve Oregon cheerleaders also appeared. WOW! Behind us- near the end zone - were about 700 Oregon fans. Hence, the cheerleaders were there to "Fire em up!"

I was spellbound: hypnotized by these yellow-clad, gorgeous knockouts: They all had "cheerleader" legs - unlike the stumpy-legged, hoggish OSU cheerleaders - picked for their "acrobatic" agility.

Instantly, Murph and I realized that we had the "best seats in the house." No need for binoculars. The Oregon cheerleaders had changed our "focus" away from the game.

Final score? A nail biter! OSU Bucks 59... Oregon Ducks 16 - another hapless, visiting, opening-day underdog. I can't remember watching a single play. In October, I got a letter from Frank - his uncle Tony had bought him a used tri-power 64 GTO convertible 4-speed.

A '64 GTO

I couldn't believe it! Ever since high school, I'd dreamed of riding in a tripower 64 GTO. In 6th period study hall, Dwight Patterson and I would draw pictures of 64 GTOs.

When Red Barn opened in spring 64, Frankie Malone and I were so obsessed with riding in a tripower GTO, it literally had taken over our lives. And why not? There was no greater thrill. Nothing more fun than the neck-snapping, mind boggling acceleration of a 64 GTO; with 3 deuce carbs! I first rode in it during Thanksgiving vacation. But Market St was all slippery. "Game postponed on account of sleet." Christmas break brought more inclement weather. By the spring quarter, I was fed up COMPLETELY with dormitory life. Pledging a fraternity, I then moved into the "frat" house. Smart move. As Martin Luther King would say...."FREE at LAST." No more despicable dorm nurds: Liberated forever from the travails of dorm life! Immediately, I found a "kindred spirit." It was my "pledge brother"- Bob Prosser (Chillicothe, Ohio); who drove an azz-hauling, aquamarine 1966 4-speed SS 396 Chevelle - A genuine factory freak. What a fun and unbelievably fast car!

Bobby was a "mad dragster" like me. But unlike me, a slacker in required academic pursuits. He flunked out. Gone after spring quarter.

Arriving home for summer vacation, i'd go cruisin' in Frank's mighty GTO convertible. What an incredibly fun car!

Opening the hood was part of the GTO mystique: THREE 2-barrel Rochester carbs, sitting atop a Pontiac 389 cube high-compression V8: pure DYNAMITE on 4 wheels.

"G-R-ROOOOOOOOOM!"

Whenever Frank punched the throttle - kicking in those 3 deuce carbs- his little GTO would violently fishtail down the street - leaving a screaming, smoking trail of molten rubber!

Pedestrians gaped in astonishment. Old people called the cops. We'd be laughing like hyenas. Whole neighborhoods went up in blue tire smoke! It was more fun than you could believe!

Frank's little GTO proved to be a BIG attention getter. Everywhere we stopped, people would appear - asking..."Is that tripower? Can you lift up the hood? Is that a Hurst shifter? etc. Frank's goat accelerated like it had after-burners. Violently your neck would snapback; your eyes wide with astonishment. Never could one imagine such an electrifying experience. One night (early July) we were cruising up Market Street - top down: then we saw a billboard..."Visit the Annual St. Dominic's Church Festival - running July 6- July 14. Mahoning Valley's Biggest Summer Celebration."

"And away we GO!"

Walking into St. Dominic's festival...WOW. It was mobbed. Well-tanned "bronze" ladies - wearing sundresses - everywhere. The ultimate venue for "people-watching." Walking up to really cute redhead, I gave her my best line..."Do you have a sister who goes to Ohio State?" (it was my great "door-opener")

Just as we began a lively conversation, her squatty-body, jealous friend YANKED her away.

Nice try.

Next "up to the plate" was Frank. (he wouldn't strike out). He'd spotted a blonde; with contrasting streaks in her hair. An ABSOLUTE knock-out (i.e.) long hair and long shapely legs.

"Love at first sight." Naturally, feelings were mutual:

Not surprisingly, I saw very little of Frank for awhile - bitten by the "love bug."

Weeks later; an unfamiliar car pulled into my driveway: a black 66 Corvette stingray; with the classic "fast-back" roofline.

A '65 Corvette Stingray

I feared the worst. It was true: Frank was behind the wheel...with a shet-eatin' grin on his face. I sensed calamity. It was the "end of the line." Frank had SOLD his iconic GTO!

Instantly, my world was shattered! I thought..."FRANK...what in the world would compel you to DO THIS?" His Corvette had a 327 cubic inch engine - nothing at all compared to his 389 tripower GTO.

His corvette was cramped. It rattled. It bounced. It was noisy. When it rained, it would LEAK! Worst of ALL...no more thunderous GTO GROWL.

Frank's 327 Stingray lacked torque. No head snapping acceleration.

The radio was terrible. It was like being jammed into a sardine can. No hip room.

The road noise and harsh ride were impossible 'to get used to."

Why Corvettes were popular was beyond my comprehension. I kept praying...Oh please God, PLEASE - let me wake up from this nightmare!

Unbelievably, Frank's vette could barely burn rubber; but it did "corner."

First time on Market street - EVERYTHING had changed. Guy in a blue, nasty-sounding 67 SS Chevelle pulled up next to us: but what could Frank do? - driving his not-so-FAST Corvette stingray-lacking any "sting" at all.

I knew - and Frank knew - he'd acted TOTALLY irrational! (i.e) COMPLETELY outta his MIND! Why in the world would he give up a car that was so unbelievably exciting - and super FAST? It was like trading away a funny, talking, green jungle parrot; for a tiny, yellow CHIRPING canary. (tweety-tweet) Of course, he'd never own up to it. Getting Frank to admit he was wrong was about as likely as Niagara Falls going dry. His tripower GTO was always some new adventure. Cars challenging at red lights. Blowing them all away.

It was ALL so obvious. Frank - being totally pussy-whipped - bought the car for his vapid, blatantly STUPID, "air-headed" girlfriend: the proverbial dumb blonde; who'd go "ga-ga" at the sight of ANY guy driving a Corvette.

Ironically - not long afterwards - Frank and his blonde hottie "broke up."

Through all the years thereafter, NEVER would Frank admit to his incredibly foolish blunder.

Worst of all, it was I who felt the greater loss. Imagine the horrible effect on me - the world's number one GTO fanatic. Like the death of cherished family pet - never could I forget. Damm: what a fun car. Pure excitement. But no more.

It spelled the end for having fun on Market street. No more heart-pounding street races. No more "molten rubber" - burning down side streets.

It was like that old BB King hit blues song..."The Thrill is Gone"

Chapter 13

AUTUMN- 1967: Ohio State University

I was walking back from my classes to my fraternity house: I saw a glistening brand new 67 GTO in the driveway.

A '67 GTO

Then I saw Mark Hyland (Springfied OH) - carrying a can of "tire gloss."

"Wow Mark, is this your GTO?"

"Sure is! It's got 335 horsepower," said Mark proudly. Naturally, my FIRST order of business (bid-ness) was to get a look-see under the hood.

Pontiac's all-new 400 cubic inch V8 was -supposedly -a big improvement vs. last year's disastrous 389 GTO motor. The 67 GTO came with either a 4-barrel standard 335 hp; or a 360 hp high-performance version: but where was the iconic GTO 3-deuce TRIPOWER?

It was disastrous! A newly-announced GM corporate policy BANNED multiple carburetors for all GM cars; except the Corvette. Obviously, this was aimed directly at Pontiac's tripower GTO.

Insanity! How utterly STUPID! Were they attempting to make the GTO a "safer car" to drive? It was preposterous. What were these brain dead, GM executives thinking?

Did they not realize what they'd done? It was like Disneyland closing "Frontierland." Papa John's banning pepperoni. Campbell's discontinuing chicken noodle.

Kraft no longer producing macaroni'n cheese. Cutting off the electricity to Times Square at night. Just what was their POINT?

Ask ANYONE who drove a GTO: first thing people would ask…"Is that tri-power?" Ya got three deuces under that hood?" To me, it was a calamity: something I'd never "get over."

Meanwhile, Mark had "polished up" his Rally II wheels. His stunning metallic blue GTO was indeed a head-turner! But was it FAST? Could it haul azz?

Said Mark…"let's go for a spin."

Starting it up, Mark was beaming with pride. A born show-off, he would now demonstrate to me - a hard core street racer - what his new GTO "could do."

After letting it warm up, we backed out of the driveway - heading to Summit Ave; a wide one-way street; a perfect "test track."

Immediately, it was "pedal to the metal!"

"G-R-R-R-R-R"...Going down Summit, Mark's GTO actually did growl - sounding like a mean machine.

But where was the TORQUE? My head did NOT snap back! Despite all the noise and effort, Mark's new GTO ran as if there were a load of slag in the trunk... a pitiful DOG!

I was shocked. Mark's car sounded like a demon; but ran like a station wagon. It was just plain slow....a slow-poke GTO! Pontiac's all-new 400 motor was a joke. A big ZERO!

Bob Prosser's 396 Chevelle would've stoned Marc's GTO by at least 5-6 car lengths. Bobby had been my pledge brother back in spring quarter '67. But having flunked out of school, Bobby was no longer around.

Having no concept of a really FAST car, Mark acted like his goat was a real barn burner. Looking over at me - with his impish grin - he kept asking...So whattya think, Sandy...whattya think?"I wanted to tell Mark his car was a dog sled; but I decided to leave well enough alone. Marc's pastoral hometown, Springfield (western) Ohio - unlike Youngstown - wasn't exactly drag-city USA.

A '66 396 Chevelle

Mark NEVER had been in a street race in his entire life. In bucolic, farm-town Springfield, I figured there were as many tractors as muscle cars.

Suddenly...I got a terrific BRAINSTORM: Why not design a TRI-POWER John Deere 12-speed (i.e.) a "muscle tractor." Imagine: Tractor pulls were now "OUT." Tractor racing would be IN!

Perhaps even spawn the all-new sport of "professional tractor drag-racing." ESPN at trackside - covering all the events.

As we drove around, Mark's face was beaming with pride: he ABSOLUTELY loved his new GTO:

Mark could care less about not having the "fastest car around. "Everyone pointing at us driving by: I could read their lips..."Look at that beautiful goat!"

Obviously Marc was thrilled; so I figured, let him be happy. No sense in me "raining on his parade."

Nevertheless - I kept remembering my former pledge brother, Bob Prosser - and his screaming 4-speed, 66 SS 396 Chevelle. It was incredibly fast; and such FUN to ride in. Bob Prosser was a"kindred" spirit - just like ME: a mad dragster; who actually went LOOKING for someone to RACE. Not surprisingly, "dapper" Bobby Prosser soon became known by the fraternity brothers as... "Our super-stud new pledge." Sorority ladies took notice: Easily, Bobby was the best-dressed guy in our "pledge" class; with a wardrobe near equal to that of a small retail men's shop. His closet - completely overloaded.

One day I was in my room - struggling awkwardly to "tie my necktie." Seeing this, Bobby quickly retrieved one of his elegant ties, and proceeded to teach me..."how to tie a Windsor knot."

After about 10 minutes of patient tutoring, Bob said..."There. Now you can tie a Windsor."

SAVED!

All my life I'd been forced to wear those classless, useless "clip on neck ties." God how I despised them!

FLASHBACK: I remembered way back when I was four: Mom was dressing me for my picture with Santa Claus. After a really nice pair of new pants and a new white shirt, she unwrapped a new clip-on necktie. Ugh. How I hated it. It just didn't belong.

Then, about 13 years later, Mom took me to the JC Penny store in the Liberty plaza- to pick out my senior class-picture wardrobe.

After choosing a sporty pair of "Towncraft" beige slacks; next would be a sharp, black "Towncraft" sport coat. But then I saw Mom run up to the register, with a (GASP) crappy, polyester, red clip-on TIE! (yeck)

Gravely disappointed, I knew deep down inside, that whenever I would look at my high school yearbook; first thing I would look for is that dreadful clip on necktie: It would become ETERNAL!

But even to this day, I thank my lucky stars to have known Bobby Prosser: What would I have done without him?

Two weeks later - after fall fraternity rush- our new "pledge," Danny Fitzpatrick- from Louisville, Kentucky- drove a sharp, white 66 GTO coupe: Automatic on the console transmission.

Everyone liked Fitz - a smooth-as-velour, laid back guy.

Fitz was the "too cool for school" type. Also a natural born lady killer.

Plus, he came from a family with big bucks! (i.e.) his dad was part-owner of a Kentucky whiskey distribution network.

If one wanted to start a charm school, Danny could be your basic curriculum! With just a bit of a Kentucky "twang" in his voice, ladies found him irresistible.

But wait...there's MORE! Danny - former band member in high school - could play a mean electric guitar: "Can't get no SATISFACTION."

Danny could play it like he was Keith Richards!

Even more amazing: Fitz - rather than the proverbial "snob" - was a genuine nice guy; he'd do anyone a favor. Can you picture someone who was 1/2 James Bond; and the other half "Wally" from "Leave it to Beaver?" That was Danny.

It was virtually impossible NOT to like Fitz: Nothing seemed to phase him at all. But WHO can be PERFECT at all times? Within one month- after moving into the fraternity house – Fitz had become mired in a harrowing love triangle: It was Mary Lynne (Delta Gamma sorority) with the super hot legs, and "come hither" voice; versus Caroline (Pi Beta Phi); who was super hot – head to toe- with a temper to match.

Of course, both ladies suspected one-another: One night - hearing commotion- I emerged from my room; just in time to see Fitz frantically pulling Mary Lynne toward the back stairwell.

Then, not even two minutes later, over the house intercom..."Dan Fitzpatrick...guest in the first floor lounge."

Dashing downstairs - opening the lounge door: guess who? Caroline - angrily tapping her long fingernails on the piano. WOW: just like a TV soap opera! Only this was FOR REAL!

But leave it to Fitz: within two weeks, Danny- always the smooth-talker - cleverly had everything smoothed over! He'd met Susan, a knockout blonde -a pledge from Kappa Kappa Gamma.

Although I knew 66 GTOs were dogs, curiosity got the best of me: Perhaps his '66 GTO was actually FAST! Improbable; but not impossible. There was but one way to find out...take a ride.

A ride? Instead, "Mr. Cool" Danny handed me his keys..."Go ahead. Take it for a spin." He was talking on the corridor phone, with "hot" Susie- not wanting any distraction.

Maneuvering Danny's white GTO out of the parking lot, I had high hopes: It was automatic, 4-barrel, with 335 horse power.

Immediately I headed up to Summit...dying with anticipation: GOING FAST! My elixir. My pulse was pounding! I was planning on lighting up his tires- putting the pedal to the metal! Then, smell blue tire smoke. The snapping back of my head...flying down the street!

Yeah, dream on. Unbelievable! Fitz's 66 goat turned out to be a certified, blue-ribbon PIG - even SLOWER than Marc Hyland's 67 GTO.

What a fool was I - thinking that Danny's 66 GTO could be any different from every other 66 hoggy GTO. After not even ten minutes, I was bored. I went back - gave Danny the keys. He gave me a quick nod, and went back to his call.

Thoroughly dismayed, I'd given up all hope in Pontiac..."Will there ever be another really fast GTO?"

I just couldn't shake those indelible memories: Cousin Mona's incredible 65 GTO; and Frankie Malone's awesome 64 tri-power goat.

Yeah. Good luck on ever seeing cars like that again.

In my never-ending search for another really EXCITING GTO, my road ahead appeared to be a complete dead end - totally dependent on some farty old GM executives; who forever might prohibit another fast GTO. Hence, I began to pray:

"Please, almighty God! Please deliver me another exciting GTO!"

Amen.

Chapter 14

JUNE 1968:

- After I wrapped up my spring quarter at OSU - Man, was I ever in need of a summer break!

- No more dreaded CHEMISTRY labs. No more horrible chemistry TESTS!

- No more all-night cramming for exams.

- Heading back home to Youngstown, I was ridin' in STYLE - driving a prestigious, majestic, 59 Electra.

- After my Aunt Edna bought her new Cadillac coupe DeVille, she gave her old Buick to me.

- Finally...I had my own "luxury" ride to get back 'n forth from OSU.

- I then recalled my first time driving the Electra to Columbus - pulling into my fraternity house driveway - and the warm "brotherly" reception that followed:

- "Sandine! Get that horrendous piece of sh*t out of our driveway; and don't park it anywhere NEAR the (fraternity) house!"

- Even worse than the Buick's exterior, was the INTERIOR. The back seat stank horribly of doggy odor:

- It was from "Buffy," Aunt Edna's cherished mongrel dog; that had never been groomed in its entire life.

- Of course, Aunt Edna would never go ANYWHERE without precious Buffy - panting happily away on its doggy blanket in the back seat.

- But bad smell and all, I had no complaints: No longer would I have to "round trip" on the wonderful Greyhound bus - seated amongst the aristocrats; the travel mode of the rich and famous!

- "Take the bus. Leave the driving to us." So went the greyhound slogan, used on radio and TV ads.

- Nevertheless, after a grueling spring quarter, I was terribly sleep-deprived. I felt totally burned out. Weak. Exhausted. Kaput.

- Dad said I looked terrible: Mom could see the dark circles under my eyes.

Then, SHOCKING news about my brother Jimmy; who'd recently TOTALED the Bonneville - driving all-buzzed-up on 3.2 beer. (He'd driven it into a deep ditch).

WOW: No more Bonneville? Mom was looking for a new one...waiting on the insurance check.

Next Sunday, I nearly fainted at church: Had a high fever; with a nasty sore throat. Monday brought an urgent trip to our family physician. I was diagnosed with severe mononucleosis. 4-6 weeks total bed rest lay ahead. Indeed, "mononucleosis" was even WORSE than it sounded! The sore throat pain was unbearable. I forced myself to drink water. Eating was near-impossible. When Frank came to see me, he said I looked like a ghost. I'd lost at least 15 pounds. A week later, my sister Carol Jean came into my bedroom: "Mom's home with the new car!" Dragging myself to the side door, I looked out and WOW...a shiny new 68 GTO convertible in the driveway! This car was GORGEOUS! Verdoro green. Beige top. White interior. And it did indeed have the smooth-shifting GM turbo-hydramatic transmission. Week after 4th of July, I actually felt well enough to take the new GTO out for a "test ride." But this goat seemed slow to me; there wasn't any TORQUE.

A '68 GTO Convertable

Nevertheless, I decided to head out to Market street. It was usually "dead" on Sunday night; but not tonight.

Going up Market, two teenage girls - about 17 - pulled alongside, and began shrieking..."WOW...nice car!"

They were actually decent-looking. No prom queens. But they seemed excited.

Continuing up Market, they remained right alongside - saying..."Pull over...pull over."Hey...why not talk a bit? Curiously,

I pulled over. Parked in some church parking lot, they both came running up to the GTO: "Nice car...you're cute! Is this yours?" "Nope...this is my Mother's GTO." Eagerly they began asking questions - wanting to know ALL about me. "Yup. I'm a sophomore at Ohio State. Yeah, I'm in a fraternity" (blah-blah blah - blah). They gave me their names and phone numbers.

After making the obligatory false promise..."Yeah, I'll call you next week," I headed back home. I just did not feel well enough for cruising around - especially in a new car that "wasn't broken in." Next Friday night - in the GTO- Frankie and I were driving out Market Street. It had just turned dark.

We were waiting at a red light: Then, a black 68 SS 396 4-speed Chevelle pulls alongside in the left lane. Two "greasers" aboard. (skinny was driving...chubby riding shotgun).

A '68 SS Chevelle

Their Chevelle looked grimy...neglected; with a dent in its right front fender.

These 2 greasers were chuckling merrily away; like they were "high." The driver was smiling at me; a "smart-azz" type of smile - wearing his perspiration-stained, white T-shirt. A real trendsetter.

Chubby, riding shotgun, was about 19 - looking like he hadn't bathed in a week; give or take a day or two. Even worse: he had pitted acne all over his complexion. What a pair! 2 smart-azz punks, in their white-trash Chevelle. Obnoxiously, they loudly began hooting away..."ALL goats are pigs! Ha-ha-ha! C'mon man...Race that hoggy GTO! Ho-ho. Yuk-yuk" etc. I looked over at Frank: "Well, are you gonna race THEM? I sensed impending doom. I felt like Custer descending into Little Big Horn. Light changes. Then, total disaster: The SS rocketed out of the hole! Despite having the GTO floored, the Chevelle effortlessly pulled away to five car lead, before we both had to stop at the next red light.

I knew what was coming: "All goats are pigs!" They both kept repeating it - over 'n over. Chubby was beside himself with laughter - pointing derisively at the GTO. The driver was knee-slapping and chuckling away.

- A more humbling, demeaning experience could NOT be imagined!

- It was all so embarrassing...so exasperating.... infuriating!

Frank - shaking his head- kept saying..."this goat needs help." Then, more trouble ahead at another red light: Stopped in the left lane was a blue 67 Dodge Coronet RT.

A '67 Cornet RT

With a monster, 440 Commando V8 as standard, these cars were practically unbeatable - packing 375 wild horses under the hood. Looking over, the driver had a "butch" haircut; thick, muscular neck - probably a linebacker or defensive end. I could plainly hear "Journey to the Center of Your Mind" (Amboy Dukes) blasting loudly from his radio. He looked straight forward; but was smirking with laughter. I could easily read his mind..."all goats are pigs." When the light changed, I floored it - actually taking a brief lead! Very brief. Then I hear this thundering VR-O-

O-O-O-M noise, as the RT goes streaking by! In no time, he had a seven car lead...at least half the block!

DAMMIT! Humiliated again! What a horrible, sickening feeling. I felt letdown. Mom's GTO was indeed, a pig; or perhaps a sea turtle.

Even worse, was just how BADLY I was getting blown away - running five, six, even seven car lengths behind!

I kept thinking..."What the hell's wrong with Mom's new goat?" Rather than a 400 cube, 350-horse standard GTO engine, Mom's goat ran like there was a squirrel on a treadmill under the hood (renewable energy). I was steaming like a boiled lobster - getting totally demolished at red lights!

Said Frank (sympathetically): "Lets race my Vette. Maybe you'll win for a change."

It was a longshot. Frank's 66 Stingray was no killer. But it wasn't all that slow either. It was well past 1 AM when we both lined up on a deserted 5th Avenue, on the northside. Going on "three"- Frank's corvette immediately pulled away - at least 7 cars ahead; after only TWO blocks! AARGH...not again! As I drove up alongside him, Frank was trying his best not to laugh TOO loudly- saying sarcastically..."that was close!"

Just great. Even my best buddy couldn't resist "rubbing salt into the wound."

OUCH!

Indeed; the whole damm night had been like a horrible dream; and it wasn't on Elm St. It was truly "a Nightmare on Market Street."

Chapter 15

AUGUST- 1968:

After getting completely DEMOLISHED that previous Friday night, I HATED Mom's new GTO - vowing NO more street racing! Despite its 400 cubic inch engine, and 350 horses, it was a squealing PIG! So damm SLOW!

What was worse than losing on Market street? It would "stick in my craw." (yowch) Mom's GTO was a great car to drive around in - until you exceeded 45 MPH; then, it would begin stalling, jerking; with mysterious, even terrifying noises coming from under the hood!

Such a fun car: it was indeed a "haunted GTO."

Then, a few days later...a DEAD battery...a car barely TWO months old. Mom and I drove out to the Pontiac dealership: Turns out it was a defective alternator.

HOWEVER: alternators costa plenty - a very pricey replacement part. Ergo, the service manager became "Stonewall Jackson"... claiming it was "nothing serious." We drove home; without further incident.

That next day, Mom's goat began "acting up." Out to the dealership again. They assured Mom the car would be properly repaired - at no charge.

Next day, we got the GTO back. I decided to give it another road test. It failed miserably. Electrical problems in any car could spell ENDLESS trouble. Every time I floored it, the GTO continued to jerk violently...it was that damm alternator!

Obviously, this shyster Pontiac dealer figured that to please just ONE dissatisfied customer, it was not worth installing a new alternator.

Ergo, the "stonewall" went higher - even higher. No tangible explanations were forthcoming at all.

Other than hiring legal counsel, we were stuck with a "lemon-flavored" goat (although a beautiful one).

Soon thereafter, fate would intervene: Last Saturday of every August, Frank and I always went to Saint Christine's annual church festival: a hugely-popular "destination spot" for west side lovely ladies.

That Saturday afternoon, I headed for downtown - looking for new shoes. I wanted to put my "best foot forward." My sister always told me..."FIRST thing a lady notices, are the shoes."

While shopping at a department store, I met Karen DeAngelo - waiting by the front exit for her ride home. Being an extrovert, I began an animated conversation with this alluring young lady.

We began to really "hit it off."

She had just graduated high school: and seemed really impressed! I was talking about Ohio State; that I was in a fraternity - studying pre-med (blah blah blah) etc.

But all too soon, her ride showed up. Always a bungler with the ladies, I'd FORGOTTEN to get her phone number. I called information - number unlisted.

But I remembered her saying she lived in Austintown - not too far from St. Christine's. Hence, it was 99% probable that she'd be at the festival that night. 7 pm... dressed casual but "cool"-

wearing my new shoes - I was ready to rock 'n roll! Driving the GTO, I picked up Frank. Oddly, he had a tense, worried facial expression. Entering the car, he dropped a bombshell: No festival? Instead, we'd be going to Waterford Park; 45 minutes away, in Chester, West Virginia; where all the horse race junkies would go to lose their money.

ME: What about St. Christine's? There'll be tons of chicks there!"

Frank: "My dad gave me money to bet on some horses that are running tonight."

"But Frank..."

"WERE GOING TO WATERFORD. My Dad got a reliable tip on the daily double... We're going to win a lot of money. Just drive."

I was trapped.

Whenever Frank got in one his "moods" it was futile to argue. He always ended up getting his way.

Driving to the track, I realized that I probably would never see Karen DeAngelo again. Damm. She had the legs of a model with the face of an angel.

My failure to get her phone number would haunt me for quite some time.

Riding with the top down seemed to cheer me up a little. It was PERFECT convertible weather! Waterford park actually proved to be a very classy place: Very pastoral. Lots of trees. I never had been in West Virginia. I didn't see any hillbillies like I was expecting. Frank was in a panic..."Hurry up. We can't miss the first race. Park right here." (we were close to the main entrance).

"No. This is VALET parking...it's three bucks."

"Park here! We're late!"

Reluctantly, I surrendered the keys, and paid three bucks to this puny cretin, who'd park the GTO. He seemed rather sneaky. But something wasn't right. Why didn't he ask me to put up the convertible top? Would he be watching the car till we returned?

I hated the idea of entrusting the car keys with this sinister little weasel.

I just hoped that Frank knew what the hell he was doing. He'd been there before with his Dad - a die-hard horse junkie.

Frank seemed frantic - literally running toward the grandstand floor - convinced that his Dad's so-called "hot tip" would lead to a big payoff.

For me, I was amused. NO ONE ever made a living betting horses. Minutes before the first race, Frank had a list of horses, and money given to him by his father: Said Frank..."Okay, here's 10 bucks. Go to the window. I want Army Boots in the first race, and Black Magic in the second...that's five tickets for the double...hurry up!"

I was in the back of the line, waiting at the betting window: Then, quite remarkably, I saw a familiar face: it was Lou Yakovucci, a bricklayer who once worked for Dad.

"Yak!" He came over to my line and stood behind me - all excited!

"Listen Ricky, bet on the 3 horse in the first; and the 5 horse in the second. You'll win for sure!"

"How do you know?"

"Just listen to me. I've been doing this for years. Both these horses like a WET track" (it had rained heavily the previous night).

Now THAT made sense! I decided to take Yak's advice. As I got to the window, it was just before post time. "For the double, I want five on 7-1, and one on 3-5."

Yeah... I already had the lingo down. I felt like a real pro. Rushing back to Frank, I became EXCITED! Yak's favorites were long shots. Just before the horses broke, I looked at my "3-5" ticket.

I'd bet on "Slipton Fell" in the first race, and "Phantom Gun" in the second. Frank looked tense. His ten bucks was like a hundred in today's money. For me, I figured for two bucks...hey, what if I won?

The announcer was smooth and emotionless- methodically calling out the horses' names. When the horses broke, people began jumping around; as if experiencing epileptic seizures.

Around the first turn, I could hear distinctly... "and Slipton Fell is moving up on the outside." Wow! Immediately, I began to jump up and down!

By the far turn, again I heard distinctly..."Slipton Fell is second." The announcer said..."And Slipton Fell wins going away!" I was jubilant. I won! But Frank was bent over - holding his hands on top of his head...."DAMMIT...I didn't have it." So enraged was Frank, I actually moved about 5 feet away. Even worse, if I acted happy, he probably would've chased me out to the parking lot! (misery loves company). At the beginning of the second race, as the horses paraded by, I got a good look at "Phantom Gun." This particular horse was so shiny black, it appeared to look blue.

It stood tall and looked as if it was ready to run. When the horses broke from the gate, Phantom Gun took the lead and won going away! Another horse who thrived on a muddy track.

This was getting easy. Yak and his two long shots made me 89 dollars richer ($800 in today's money) By the third race, Frank had relaxed a bit. There was the perfecta to bet in the 5th and 6th races. Again, Frank had his Dad's instructions.

Just before the 5th race, Frank took out his list, gave me money, and which horses to play. Walking toward the betting window, I was looking for Yak. He was in the corner - looking down at his racing form - pen in hand.

"Hey Yak. I won the double! Thanks! Who do you like in the perfecta?"

After betting EXACTLY the way Yak advised, I decided to part with two additional bucks, to cover Frank- in case I won. I didn't want to drive him home as a total loser...He had a TEMPER.

The perfecta was easier to win. If your horse won, or placed second or third, you won money.

As luck would have it, it would be one of the few times in my life where I actually WON. I owed it all to Yak. After collecting an additional 41 dollars after the 6th race, I was up 129 bucks! Big money for 1968. Frank acted as if his 41 dollars - thanks to me - was a big deal! We decided to quit while ahead.

Walking out the exit, we were singing, laughing and joking away. We had walked for quite a distance; when suddenly, we realized we were WAY beyond the valet parking area.

Walking around the vast parking lot, the GTO seemed to have vanished. We walked back up toward the main entrance. The valet parking area was deserted.

I began to panic. All the valet parking jockeys were GONE. There was no one around.

I asked "Frank...."Have you ever parked valet before?"

"No."

Instantly, I realized the GTO had been stolen! Obviously, the work of a criminal, auto-theft racket.

I knew that weasel - who'd parked the car - seemed untrustworthy. It was that 'look" on his face that had unnerved me. Walking back inside, we were directed to security. About 10 minutes later, the police arrived - a stolen car report filed.

The track manager showed up- apologizing profusely. He said we'd be driven home - right to our front doors...and "Our insurance will take care of everything."

They actually came through. The manager was aware of the track's reputation. Numerous people from Youngstown went there. As promised, a taxi drove us home. Arriving 2 am, I had mixed emotions: Would Mom be upset? As it turned out she was completely relieved. We had insurance. Waterford park had insurance. Said Mom..."We'll rent a car for now, or use your

Father's (new) truck." In one fell swoop, the GTO dilemma had been solved! Police reported some auto theft ring - operating out of Pittsburgh - had stolen the GTO.

Ten days later, Mom opened up an official-looking envelope:

It was from Waterford park: a cashiers check for FORTY TWO HUNDRED DOLLARS! Well in excess of what we'd paid for the nightmarish 68 GTO.

QUOTE:

"All's well that ends well."

William Shakespeare

Chapter 16

MAY 1969: OHIO STATE UNIVERSITY campus

It was around 2 pm. I was walking on North Oval Drive, when a sleek, black, 69 GTO drove by:

Wow! Was it ever a gorgeous car! It looked amazing. It sounded "gutsy." I was stunned. What an improvement over the 68 GTO!

Later on, I was flipping through an issue of "Hot Rod" magazine; with the all-new 1969 GTO "JUDGE" on its front cover.

A '69 Judge GTO

The JUDGE? What a stupid name! Who's idea was that?

Why not call it "the SHERIFF?" Or the "Sergeant-at Arms?"

Carousel red (orange) was the only available Judge color. Flashy racing stripes running down each side - conveying a "high-impact" message (i.e.) "Don't MESS with me, BRO!" The Judge looked like a real, down 'n dirty street fighter; with its RAM AIR 400 motor - 366 horses... open hood scoops. Close-ratio 4 speed gears. Pontiac had designed the Judge to look

IMPOSING...FOREBODING; and succeeded. Other "Judge" innovations were its hood-mounted tach; with a rear deck spoiler. A hood-mounted tachometer? How absurd!

What if it's raining? Why not keep it dash-mounted? What if the driver was near-sighted? What about vandalism? How dumb.

After final exams, I was riding home for summer vacation in a 69 427 Corvette - driven by "the Snake" - Allen Sellers - who lived in Beaver Falls PA; 35 miles from Youngstown. Snake was my "devilish" fraternity brother - always the joker - always fun to be around.

The proverbial "spoiled rich kid," Snake's father owned a thriving appliance store in downtown Beaver Falls. Exiting his car, Snake yelled to me..."Don't forget to come down in August for my summer pool party...they'll be tons of chicks."

"I'll be there for sure Snake! See ya in August!" As I walked into the house, my sister greeted me: "Mom and Jeff went to go pick up OUR NEW car." Now that was BIG news! I pictured another Bonneville. Not another GTO.

While scavenging through the fridge - out in the driveway - I heard a deep-throated, powerful rumbling sound. The unmistakable "exhaust note" of a high-powered muscle car.

I looked out to the driveway - WOW - I saw a glistening, brand new, gorgeous, verdoro green 69 GTO convertible! I was "floored!" Couldn't believe my eyes!

A '69 GTO convertible

Mom was pressing the power button- putting the top down. My brother Jeff, was attaching the "boot" - concealing the retracted top. Mom's new GTO was DROP DEAD gorgeous! A jaw-dropper!

SHARPEST convertible in town!

Said Mom: "It was the best looking car on the lot. I fell in love with it at first sight!"

Looking inside, was a factory-installed 8-track (tape-player). Just pop in a cartridge and simultaneously play 4 different songs! YES! A fun and fast FAMILY car! A convertible! Was I dreaming?

Walking up to Frank's house, his black corvette was in the driveway. He laughed when I told him about Mom's new 69 goat. Frank was not impressed..."Another pig GTO?"

I had no rebuttal. Since 1966, GTOs were universally referred to as "pigs." Objects of ridicule by those who were street racers. Next Monday night I decided take a test spin in Mom's new goat. Driving the new GTO, it seemed REALLY FAST. Uncanny "pick-up."

This 69 "had balls." Touch that gas pedal and go charging down the highway! This goat had torque-aplenty!

Best of all was the 8 track tape-player; an awesome feature.

I was cruisin.' Singing. Smiling...enjoying: Such a fun car to drive!

"Should I put down the top?"

Suddenly, about a mile from downtown, trouble coming up from behind: a new, blue 69 SS 396 4-speed Chevelle- two aboard - looking over at me like I was some clueless moron.

Pulling alongside, they gleefully began harassing me: "Hey man, wanna race your pig GTO? Ha-hah-ha!" Looking over at the shiny new Chevelle, I couldn't believe my eyes! Guy riding shotgun was Harry Snead - whom I DESPISED.

Snead had graduated with me in high school...was in my sophomore gym class.

Despite buck teeth, greasy hair AND freckles, Snead thought of himself as "Mr. Super Cool."

Not someone you'd invite to your birthday party. I absolutely could not stand the sight of this cretin: the very definition of a big-mouth JERK! Of course, he quickly recognized me..."Hey Sandine! C'mon man... race that pig GTO! HA-HA...Ho-ho... Yuk-yuk" etc. The driver - gunning his motor - was another brazen, smart-azz punk. We were stopped at the next red light. Snead - laughing like a hyena - looked over - yelling..."C'mon Sandine. Race that pig GTO. You CHICKEN!"

Light goes green! V-R-ROOOOOOOM!

Immediately, Mom's GTO blasted out to a three car lead! After the automatic trans up-shifted, I began pulling away! I was AMAZED.

At 80 mph, I took my foot off the gas.

In my mirror were their headlights, maybe 6 car lengths behind. I was CERTAIN the SS driver had MISSED 2nd gear.

They pulled alongside at the next red light: Both the driver and Snead looked SHOCKED. Astonished. Snead's face was "a whiter shade of pale" (play Procol Harum song). His demonic laughing was GONE.

The SS driver looked dazed and confused. (play Led Zeppelin song)

They drove away - speechless - totally awestruck.

Days later, on Market - a black 69 SS 396 Camaro 4-speed pulls alongside - driven by some teen aged hot shot - thinking..."I'll blow away this jerk in his pig GTO" etc.

Light changes. Immediately Mom's GTO screams out to a 4 car lead, then pulls away.

Astonishing!

It was incredible! Mom's GTO could SURGE away from a green light - like a bolt shot from a crossbow! I was laughing!

At the next light, the now- humbled Mr. Hot Shot looks over... "Is that ram air?"

"Are you kidding? This is my Mother's GTO!"

Not ten minutes later - at a red light - I was next to a vitamin C orange 69 Roadrunner. The driver- about 20 - acted "unconcerned."

On his radio I could hear "GET BACK" (the Beatles) playing loudly. He pretended to ignore me. Just before the light changed, he turned down his radio...a sure indication he was ready to race.

When the light turned, I went streaking away to a 3 car lead. When the trans upshifted, I could see the Roadrunner in my mirror: he was at least 5 cars to the rear.

He slowed down and turned onto a side street.

"Hasta La Vista" sore loser!

It was official: Mom's goat was 3 and zero- incredibly FAST for a factory stock GTO!

Next Saturday morning, I went to tell Frank- sitting on his front porch- drinking coffee.

I gave him the rundown about Mom's GTO.

Frank thought I had gone plum crazy...like I was "talking shet."

"Look Frankie, if you don't believe it, we'll go out Market tonight."

Time check: 8 PM. Riding toward downtown, I kept crowing away about Mom's freaky-fast GTO.

Frank was totally skeptical- an infidel. A disbeliever.

"You'll see. This goat is unbelievably quick out of the hole."

We were stopped downtown at the red light before the Market street bridge. Pulling alongside was a dark blue 68 SS 396 Chevelle - an obvious "greaser" driving (i.e) oily hair; grimy complexion - looking unwashed.

He wore a grease-stained, white t-shirt - not of "designer" origin.

But that shaking Chevelle! - quivering like jello. The clattering, noisy idle CONFIRMED it was the dreaded L-78 option...375 horses: solid lifter camshaft. 11-to-one compression.

The nastiest Chevelle on the street.

It was a long red light. There were 'left turn' arrows. Looking over at the menacing SS, I became nervous: I actually considered 'chickening out.'

What if I got blown away? Last thing I wanted to hear from Frank..."I TOLD you so".

Light about to change. My heart pounding. I was 99% sure I was about to lose. An L-78 Chevelle was perhaps the most intimidating car one could encounter at any red light.

This was it. The light went green!

WHAA-ROOOOOM!

I stomped on the gas - Mom's GTO leaped forward with AMAZING acceleration! It was shocking!

Instantly, I had a two car lead. The thundering noise from the monster SS Chevelle was unbelievable. BRAAA-WHOO-O-O-O-O-M! Frank - looking back in amazement- said..."here he comes." Looking at the fading SS in my mirror, I said happily..."No-o-o he's not!" He lost by about 2 1/2 car lengths. However, at the next light, Mister greaser was "gracious" in defeat - he seemed like a nice guy, rather than a sore loser.

"That's a pretty good running goat ya got there. Is that ram air?"

"Nope...this is my Mother's GTO."

Ugh! Then I saw his unsightly rotted teeth- disgusting. He probably had not seen a dentist in years; or a toothbrush. YECK!

His grimy T-shirt sleeves were rolled up to his armpits. Not exactly a candidate for the next "GQ" front cover (Gentleman's Quarterly magazine).

Looking over at Frank, he said NOTHING. Of course, no way stubborn Frank would admit he'd been wrong; about as likely as the moon falling from the sky. He could be a total jerk at times.

Cleverly, he attempted to change the subject:

"Let's go back home and race my vette on Belmont."

"You sure you wanna race?"

Frank was sure. First, he needed to stop for gas.

Heading back home, I was elated. All GTOs were NOT pigs. Certainly not this one!

Arriving at Frank's house, he retrieved his keys. I followed his Vette. Destination: The 24-hour Belmont Clark gas station - greaser HQ for the north side. The huge red Clark sign was like a beacon in the night. It was catty-corner to the Red Barn. The place where all the greasers would congregate...to "shoot the breeze," about "who had beaten whom" in street races around town. Such "discussions" could go on endlessly for hours.

Frank pumped his gas. Spotting Bennie Greco- an old friend from junior high - I idled over to say hello. He appeared rather surprised to see me.

"Wow! Nice goat Ricky... Whenja get that?"

"It's my Mother's GTO."

"How's it run?"

"I just whomped a 68 Chevelle L-78 over the Market street bridge by 3 cars. Frank was riding with me."

"Yeah? What'd it look like?"

"Dark blue. Kinda rough. Guy driving was skinny, about 23. Blond hair."

"Did he have bad teeth?"

"YEAH....how did you know?"

"I know that guy! Gary Conners. And that's not a 396, it's a 427! He and his dad race cars!"

The news spread like a 5-alarm fire. Immediately, about 10 greasers encircled the GTO. They insisted I pop the hood.

"Nope. No ram air....Hard to believe you beat Conners' 427. That car really runs."

Pointing to Frank's Corvette - I said..."ask him."

The greasers looked at Mom's GTO, awestruck.

Supposedly, Conner's 427 Chevelle was the fastest car ANYWHERE around.

I followed Frank out to Belmont & Rt 304...perfect for our "big" race.

It was NO contest at all!

Frank's 66 vette ran as if powered by an energetic hamster, running its wheel: Its worn and torn 327 engine could give no more.

By the time I hit 80 mph, he was 7 cars back. His Corvette - smoking heavily, like a train locomotive.

Frank wasn't too happy about his car's performance. I said nothing - not someone who "rubs it in." Not me.

11:15 PM...plenty of time for a quick trip back to Market Street. I was elated! I felt like a captured lion, being released back into the wild! GRRRRR.

It didn't take long to locate another "victim."

Spotting a 69 Superbee headed downtown - I made a sharp u-turn. I pulled up next to the lurid yellow Dodge, with its "bumblebee" racing stripe.

Guy at the wheel was a typical greaser-type - wearing black glasses...grimy T-shirt...hair oiled up...a real trendsetter.

True to form, the greaser was laughing: I could read his mind..."Another pig GTO. I'll blow this jerk away."

I was laughing..."You're in for a big surprise, Mr. Axle Grease."

It was an instant replay: Moms GTO zoomed away from the yellow Coronet as if he had a 225 slant 6 cylinder, rather than a 383 magnum V8.

Axle grease drove off. I was low on gas. Driving back home, I was on cloud nine! - experiencing a sort of "Nirvana."

To me, Mom's GTO was gift from heaven! A car that ran FASTER than HELL!

Thank the good Lord above!

Chapter 17

JUNE: 1969

It was Saturday, around noon:

I was washing Mom's GTO, when out-of-the-blue, Dominic Tondo - a greaser whom I recognized from Isaly's - pulled up to the driveway in a '62 Corvair. He was acting as a "messenger." Would I like to race his friend, Donnie Palermo; who drove a 66 tripower GTO?

Evidently, the greasers at Clark's gas station had spread the word: that a stock 69 GTO convertible had blown away Gary Conner's monster 427 SS Chevelle.

Supposedly, Donnie Palermo's 66 goat was undefeated: with 3-deuce carbs. Close-ratio 4 speed gears. Exhaust splitters. Safety-trak 3.90 gear differential (posi-traction). Transistorized ignition. The whole works. It was feared by all on the North side.

And who's Donnie Palermo? He was the "toast" of the North side! A local 'CELEBRITY' - assistant manager of the Liberty Plaza theater...the most comfortable and enjoyable theater in Youngstown. If one wanted to see the latest, first run movies, it was Liberty Plaza theater - hands down!

Best theater I've ever attended.

The management went to great lengths make you "feel at home." It was always well-attended. Patrons felt secure; none of the sleaziness of a downtown cinema. Their modern "flex" seats were so cool; like they were mounted on rollers. It was easy to get past someone to get to your seat, anywhere in the aisle.

Everyone knew Donnie Palermo; he was smooth...well-liked. Friendly. Always the perfect gentleman; and being ASSISTANT theater manager, he'd let you in FREE!

Ergo, Donnie never seemed to lack any friends!

"Nice-guy" Donnie had that "300-watt movie-star smile" that ladies found irresistible. So bright was his smile he could've become rich, just by collecting royalties appearing in TV toothpaste commercials.

"Look mom - NO CAVITIES!"

Since Dom Tondo and Donnie were best buddies - I decided...what the heck? If Palermo was serious enough to send his buddy to challenge me, then why not race?

And so, the scene was set: 1 AM, tonight, I'd meet Donnie at 5th ave and Broadway (on the north side); an absolutely IDEAL place for a big-time street race.

FLASHBACK: summer 1964. Frankie and I had walked up to the Liberty Plaza theater. We paid 75 cents admission to see "Island of the Blue Dolphin" - a totally insipid movie.

During the film, I found myself distracted by this very polite usher- wearing his spiffy red uniform - who'd escorted us to our seats.

It was indeed, service with a smile! This guy was a real pro. He'd escort newly arrived patrons to their seats. Then, he'd make that grand "here you are" gesture with a sweeping right hand- flash the bright smile - and head on over to seat another. Imagine - being impressed by some teen-aged movie usher? It was indeed, Donnie Palermo. Not only did Liberty Plaza Theater have the best ushers; they had the best in candy, pop and popcorn; always fresh. Always tasty. No stale, teeth-jarring tootsie rolls. Fresh Cracker Jacks. Just the right amount of butter on the popcorn (not soggy).

Even their stainless steel pop machine stood out. It was always immaculate. Their 7-up was world class. It was crystal clear. Your lips would smack upon tasting it. It was worth the admission, just to buy their fabulous 7-Up! YUMMM!

Another"drawing card" to Liberty Plaza theater was its "janitorial excellence." When you walked into the Men's room, it was Lysol city. Mr Clean on steroids. No fear of going into any stall. No rusty-looking fixtures. Shiny, spot free mirrors. Sanitary sinks. I figured the owner(s) had to be clean freaks!

Indeed, Donnie Palermo had carried on the theater's reputation: He was pure class!

Then I recalled two years earlier: my brother had said that he and a friend had seen "Bonnie 'n Clyde" for free...courtesy of Donnie Palermo!

That afternoon, I felt a bit uneasy...uncertain:

It was those ominous, parting words from Dominic Tondo..."he's gonna blow your doors off.... his goat's a FACTORY FREAK."

That night, 7 pm, I went to Frank's house: He was trying on his new "Nehru" jacket - preparing for some sizzling "hot" date. Frank looked upon himself as a trendsetter; always at the forefront of the latest men's fashion fads. A dashing ladies man - madly in love with a different female every month. So on this

Saturday night, I'd be riding solitaire - heading out to Market street. It was like a carnival of muscle cars...SS Chevelles. 396 SS Camaros. Superbees. Roadrunners. Charger RTs - seemingly at every other red light; and they all were "gunning" for a "pig" GTO.

68 Camaro SS convertible

It was indeed a "target-rich" environment. Time to "run whatch a brung."

For the next three hours, I zoomed up 'n down Market; as if on "fast-forward." It was like a muscle car shoot- out; and I had the highest score!

After Mom's GTO would destroy some hapless rival, I'd make a U-turn- chasing down another one - going in the opposite direction. Picture that! Total insanity! A rabid, MAD DOG behind the wheel. It seemed a fantasy. No one could even come close!

I felt invincible. UNCONQUERABLE. Alexander the Great, behind the wheel of a 69 GTO. 12:45 AM - time to head back to the north side. Would Donnie Palermo be waiting? I could care less. Ain't no way a so-called "freaky-fast" 66 goat could even come close to Mom's decimating GTO.

Then, total and complete astonishment: Driving to the north side - arriving at 5th avenue – there were no less than 150 people lining the street...as if waiting for July 4th fireworks to start.

The news about Donnie racing that night was contagious: North side people had been talking about it all that Saturday. Donnie Palermo had his own fan base! They showed up in numbers to cheer their hero!

Wow...I felt like a prize fighter about to step into the ring..."In this corner, Ricky Sandine, in a 69 GTO...400 cubic inches...350 horsepower."

Donnie appeared right on time - with a "passenger:" His drop-dead gorgeous girlfriend was sitting in his lap (quite a distraction). The 4-speed shifter at her feet.

Instantly I realized Donnie Palermo was indeed a celebrity! And apparently, so was his immaculately-clean GTO: A shiny white "pearl" color. Dazzling, shining mag wheels. Even his chrome exhaust splitters were glistening like new.

"Hooray!" People cheered when Donnie appeared - shouting..."Go Donnie...you can do it...blow this guy away" etc.

It was amazing! They should've been filming. It was something worth remembering!

I was sharing center stage with the one and only Donnie Palermo! I was laughing. I had not expected ANYTHING like this!

It was now 1 O'clock AM...time to get the show on the road. One arduous fan - wearing an NAPA (auto parts) T-shirt - offered to be flagman. But the red light would be suitable enough for a fair start. Just a lot of good-natured, spontaneous fun.

Waiting at the light, I was thinking...a really fast SIXTY SIX GTO? HAH! I'd never heard of any such thing. To me, all had been pitiful dogs: USDA-certified hogs. Suddenly, the red light jumped GREEN!

G-R-R-ROOOOOOM! Donnie's tripower carbs wailed like a tornado; my eardrums were echoing away. God was it LOUD!

Donnie's GTO was surprisingly quick out of the hole - one and half car lengths behind Mom's GTO. This 66 tri power goat was indeed a bit freaky.

Looking at my side mirror, his headlights began fading away. Mom's GTO - with a two car lead- now slowly and inevitably began pulling away. Donnie's goat had suffered its first defeat.

Post-race, most of these "ain't never been beat" losers would be spouting a litany of excuses (i.e.) I needa tune-up, etc.

But not Donnie: Driving up to me, he seemed totally unfazed; so calm, collected and cool! Youngstown's own version of Steve McQueen.

Donnie - arm arched over his sizzling hot girl friend - was indeed the "King" of Cool" on the North side! I asked Donnie..."Wanna race again?" Donnie - flashing his "movie star" smile - nonchalantly replied.. "Nope...I quit." Then he simply drove away. I was a bit surprised; even rather shocked! Never have I seen anyone so lackadaisical about LOSING a momentous street race! Especially for the first time. A sore loser he was not. Donnie wasn't trying to prove anything to the world. He didn't care all that much that he'd finally lost. So what?

But for ME? Losing would rock my foundations - because I was determined to prove to the world that all GTOs were NOT pigs!

AFTERMATH: Donnie's caravan of fans now began to hit the road. Looking over at the demoralized spectators, they seemed be taking the loss even worse than Donnie - looking totally disappointed.

Some seemed profoundly shocked - shaking their heads as they headed for home. Their hero had LOST.

But again, it did not seem to phase Donnie at all!

It was just like that popular hit tune from the late 80s, by Bob Mc Pherrin: "Don't Worry...Be Happy."

Mr. Cool, care-free Donny Palermo, could have written this song!

Occasionally, I still wonder where he is today...the amazing Donnie Palermo!

Chapter 18

JULY 1969:

IMAGINE THIS:

Spending 3 wonderful years at Ohio State; in "glamorous" (hick-town) Columbus; where TRACTOR pulls were "social events."

Then, I'd come home to good ol' Youngstown, and - ah yes - Market Street! The LAND of MILK 'n HONEY for drag racers!

And best of all, in Youngstown- NO bullying, militaristic COPS- like the ones in cow-town Columbus – prowling around on their Harley motorcycles.

Columbus cops were ubiquitous - literally transforming the State Capitol into a "police state."

To me, Columbus was like living on a far-distant planet (i.e.) Pluto. Uranus...or lovely Saturn.

Hence, upon ANY break from school, I'd go back to Youngtown; where everything seemed "NORMAL."

But Columbus did have something FABULOUS Youngstown did NOT:

White Castle CHEESEBURGERS! (i.e.) grenade burgers. After getting stupefyingly drunk at a frat party; what could be more satisfying (or addicting) than woofing down a bag-full of gut-busting, greasy "sliders."

YUM-M-M!

One day, I received a surprise phone call: it was Richie DePizzo: my best buddy fraternity brother - asking me how I was doing inYoungstown this summer. He lived in Lakewood; on Cleveland's west side.

"Richie D" (as he was known) was a charismatic, easy-going guy...a person who "lit up a room" whenever he appeared.

After being elected fraternity rush chairman, Richie D had been my first "pledge." A "Man for all Occasions" - wearing many hats - Richie D was my "main man." He could do it all:

Fraternity house pool shark: Handsome, suave ladies man. Private chauffeur. First rate jock. And best of all, a gifted practical joker- renowned for his infamous UPCHUCK caper...usually on a Saturday night: It went like this:

The 3rd floor (animal floor) of our frat house was mostly "single" occupancy.

However - after weekend parties - certain rooms would become "double occupancy." Amorous shrieks, giggling - easily heard from a certain room. (love was in the air) Everyone listening:

Richie - empty waste basket in hand - would stand outside the locked door, waiting for a "climactic" moment; and then pretend to THROW UP - emitting a loud, guttural "HOO-AH" "while pouring water into the empty waste basket."

Then, a most-hurried unlocking of the door..."DAMMIT! Who's BARFING out here?"

Ha-ha! Next time, get a MOTEL room cheapskate! (it's a tax write-off) Even better: Richie D (6 ft 2" 220 lbs.) could imitate Elvis, BIGTIME.

Richie D - perhaps the original karaoke performer - could mimic Elvis as if he were "the King" himself!

Using an empty pop bottle as a microphone prop - "Jailhouse Rock" playing on the house stereo - Richie would shuck 'n jive around - shoulders jerking - shuffling his feet - looking much like Elvis in his iconic, 1957 "Jailhouse Rock" video.

If Richie had been wearing a rhinestone outfit; you'd think it was Elvis himself! It sure shocked me. He had all of Elvis' mannerisms "Down to a T."

Suddenly, I had an idea! Why not check out Cleveland? Were there any drag racers prowling about the "North Coast?" (55 miles from Youngstown).

Yeah...why not find out?

I told Richie I would meet him later tonight.

TIME CHECK: 7:30 PM.

Turning into his driveway in mom's GTO convertible, Richie seemed impressed:

RICHIE: "WOW....sharp car Ricky! Is this yours?"

ME: "Nope. It's my mother's GTO. Let's go race. This goat's never been beat! You'll be amazed."

Richie: "let's put the top down." (done)

ME: "Where to?"

RICHIE: "Where to what?"

ME: "Where do we go to race? Where does everyone go?"

Richie: "The only place to race MIGHT be Clifton Blvd."

MIGHT be? Incredibly, Cleveland had nothing like Market St, or Belmont. I just couldn't fathom that Cleveland - with a population many times that of Youngstown - had no "traditional" place to street race. It seemed implausible.

Without much choice, we headed for Clifton Boulevard, around 8:15 PM.

Turning onto Clifton, it was kind of a disappointment: NOT like the bright lights of Market street on a Saturday night.

Traffic was sparse. Muscle cars nowhere to be seen. No hot shots burning rubber. We meandered - going red light to red light.

At last, some well dressed guy (late 20s) driving a silver 67 Corvette, 327 cubic inch - pulls alongside - looking deeply in thought. (probably a cheap attorney)

Light changes...and NOTHING!

Guy in the corvette was like grampa driving on Sunday; perhaps too "mature" to engage in a juvenile endeavor like street racing.

Totally UNREAL! No one racing on Clifton...or anywhere else!

To me, it was "culture shock." Where was all the "action" in the Cleveland metro area?

EVEN WORSE: no jumpin'-thumpin' bars within driving distance. Action on the North coast seemed confined to neighborhood taverns- but not much else.

Finally, it occurred to me...culturally, Youngstown – compared to Cleveland: The two cities were LIGHT years apart. Cleveland had the Indians. The Browns...a MAJOR league city.

Youngstown had the "Youngstown Hard Hats" (semi-pro football team); and class AA MINOR league baseball.

Cleveland was home to the sprawling, world renowned Case-Western University.

Diminutive Youngstown "College" had recently become Youngstown "STATE" University. Cleveland had "five star" restaurants - elegant dining.

Youngstown was all smoke-filled taverns - serving hot sausage; or a fried baloney sandwich. Peirogi dinners for "take-out."

Cleveland had an "aura of sophistication." People were polite-well educated. Affluent.

Youngstown was considered a "blue-collar-tough" ethnic town; where you would often hear the boast..."I don't take NO SHET from no-body!" (duh)

Cleveland had its own string symphony; exclusive art galleries.

Youngstown had its "famous" Mike Roncone orchestra - featuring head singer "Fuzzy Polumbo." Mike Roncone a headliner on the alto sax.

Cleveland's scenic Lake Erie shore line - attracting a plethora of leisure craft (boats) from all over North Eastern Ohio.

Youngstown- on the "pristine" Mahoning river - attracting a plethora of hungry catfish (i.e.) carp.

High school football? in Cleveland...no big thing.

Youngstown was all BITTER high school rivalries - front page news.

A "never give up on anything" attitude permeated Youngstown; the world's third largest steel manufacturing center. A town populated with "Joe Lunch-Bucket" blue-collar types; who went to church on Sunday.

At last it dawned upon stupid-dumbell me: Cleveland was like another world compared to Youngstown - where NO ONE cared one damm bit about street racing.

Ergo, it was time to say "good-by Cleveland." Exit stage right.

"See ya back at school for autumn quarter, Richie." (bon voyage)

Of course, when school resumed for fall quarter; everyone - upon seeing Richie again - wanted him to do his Elvis act for them "right now."

Soon, he realized that with being so popular - mimicking Elvis - it became a double-edged sword....a burden - happening anywhere or any time.

Imagine this: wherever Richie went, everyone wanted him to do "Elvis." (e.g.) "C'mon Richie. Do your Elvis imitation for ME."

Or...”Hey Richie.. Could you do your Elvis act for me again? It's so FUNNY. I was LMAO.”

PLEASE?

Naturally, Richie could no longer live a “normal” student lifestyle. Those “I wanna see Elvis” people could distract him at the most inopportune times.

Since he and I were best-buddy fraternity brothers, we always hung together- hitting the crowded OSU bars every FRIDAY afternoon.

Predictably, anyone who “casually” knew him, would brazenly interrupt our ongoing conversation (e.g.) “Richie! Could you do your Elvis imitation for me and my girlfriend? I told her it's the funniest thing I've ever SEEN.” (he was holding hands with his cute lady friend).

Unfortunately, people now began to get a bit too aggressive:

Picture Richie - sitting at his table, engaged in conversation; and here comes someone Richie barely knew - insisting that he do his Elvis imitation for them...RIGHT NOW.

When he walked around campus, occasionally he was “recognized.” Then came the obligatory request...”Richie, could you do a little bit of Elvis for me?”

But now that Richie had tasted a bit of fame, it would see him losing his fortune - ACADEMICALLY.

Twice, he was perilously close to “flunking out.”

And so - not wanting to see him “kicked out of OSU”- I put Richie on my personal “program” (i.e.) how to party-up bigtime” at Ohio State, by simply going to classes! Just go to class; and you'll be able to cover your azz - grade-wise. It worked! I began by making sure he attended all his classes. Richie now assumed his strange new "role"... becoming a STUDENT! He actually bought text books!

Richie didn't quite make the Dean's list; but by middle of his sophomore year, Richie had greatly improved: all of his grades heading north.

And by this time, the stale Elvis act had run its course (once you see it, you've seen it)

But old habits don't easily die: Richie, the former, numero-uno drunk in the fraternity- for some reason - restarted his old chugga-lug boozing again.

Sorority ladies began talking..."Richie DePizzo totally grossed me out at a fraternity party last Saturday night. He was unbelievably DRUNK!"

Soon, calls from sorority ladies began drying up.

Richie - once considered the "hottest guy" in the fraternity - had "relapsed." Alas, all the beer chugging had now transformed him into..."the tall guy with the beer gut!"

Worst of all: Richie now failed to notice that he was at the THRESHOLD of "alcoholism lite" (i.e.) that if one drank beer ONLY; you could not possibly be considered an actual alcoholic. Progressively, it began to get worse: Richie now went "hard core." Often after weekend parties, drunken Richie would be seen staggering down the 3rd floor corridor - bashing on every door: "Hey guys, rally time...it's only one 1 AM...the Varsity Club has a 2:30 (liquor) license: C'mon, lets go!" Predictably, some haughty SENIORS on the 3rd floor, had become really jerked-off at the boozing, obnoxious Richie - complaining to the "High Alpha" (fraternity) president.

But of course, nothing was done!

After all, most of the complainers were marathon boozers themselves! They simply were much more DISCREET about it.

QUOTE:

"Let Ye, WHO NEVER HAS SINNED, CAST THE FIRST STONE."

Chapter 19

A 1968 Dodge Superbee

JULY - 1969:

QUESTION: Have you ever been in one of those serene moods; when you feel like cruising alone - listening to your favorite music? Well, that was me, one July Saturday night.

I was driving onto the I-680 freeway from the Meridian Road ramp: no particular destination- singing merrily along with the 8-track (tape player). La-dee-dah...what a beautiful summer night! The Milky Way "was glowing from above." It was becoming dark.

Then, LOOKEE here - a navy-blue, 69 Plymouth 440 GTX - coming up in the left lane - moving alongside me: We were both going an "easy-breezy" 55 mph. Glancing over, I saw the driver; and indeed, he was the epitome of ARROGANCE - with his big-bad, 440 Super Commando V8 under his hood: the same engine found in that black, 1968 Dodge Charger RT, which "starred" in the classic 1968 action film, "BULLITT."

A '69 Plymouth GTX

NOTE: Unlike the movie - in REALITY - there was NO freak-keen way Steve McQueen's 390 Mustang could run down a 440 RT Charger on the open road.

A 440 super-Commando V8 (375 HP) was capable of head-snapping-acceleration...dazzling speeds on the top end! Nearly enough torque to pull a short passenger train.

Behind the wheel of a 440 RT Dodge, you were FEARED as one BAD mother-brother...one of fastest cars of the late 60s.

First time watching "BULLITT"- since I hated Fords- I was actually rooting for the 2 bad guys in the RT!

Although a fantastic movie - a 390 Mustang was FALSELY depicted as being dominant over an INDOMITABLE Charger RT: Pure FANTASY...about as likely as California sliding into the Pacific ocean. Looking over at this cocky GTX driver, he gave a nudge to his really pretty (knock-out) girlfriend nestled beside him: I could read his lips: "Watch me blow away this GTO."

"Oh yeah?"

Within a split-second, we both hit the throttle; almost simultaneously:

VR-R-R-O-O--O-O-O-OOOM!

Immediately, the GTX's front end leaped violently upward! The roaring/whining 440 engine sounded so darn LOUD!

I floored Mom's goat:

"GRRRRROOOOM." The trans downshifted - propelling Mom's GTO into "fast forward." It began accelerating with startling velocity!

Momentarily, we were deadlocked: Then - gathering speed - the GTO began to gradually pull away from Mr. Hot Shot; in his mighty "Gee-Tex" PLYMOUTH!

Glancing in my mirror, never could I forget his look of bewilderment; which had turned into dismay (i.e.) "WHAT THE HELL's in that GTO?"

At 100 MPH, he was a car length behind; and NOT about to give up. The embarrassment of losing before his "lady friend" compelled him to go on.

My speedometer now hit 110: still he persisted in trying to close the gap. In my mirror, he now looked TOTALLY determined: no way was he gonna lose to a GTO! Glancing at my 120 mph speedometer- the needle was wound all the way around past ZERO! It seemed surreal - like a blur: the night landscape was flashing by. At last...the driver flashed his bright lights. The race ended, with the GTX behind by 3 car lengths. We both pulled off the road. The astonished GTX driver came running up to me..."Man... my speedometer said 130; and you were pulling away!" Opening the hood I showed him the goat's 400/350 STOCK motor. He appeared to be "all shook up." But in contrast, his knockout girlfriend – primping her blonde hair in the lit-up sun visor mirror - seemed (yawn) bored by it all.

Upon departing, he looked as if he needed to change his fruit-of-the looms (i.e.) like he'd "soiled" his drawers. Can't blame him. I felt likewise...mentally "drained."

Hood up, I decided to check the all-important engine oil level: Wow...down by a HALF quart! (sniff-sniff) An overpowering, metallic burning smell was apparent; like when my electric train went off the tracks. It reminded me of when I was four - having fun with my American Flyer electric train.

This meant the GTO had nearly suffered near-catastrophic engine damage - due a sudden oil pressure DROP! Absolutely brilliant on my part. The 400 engine had been pushed to its limit - only moments away from total ruination.

Indeed: another 15/30 seconds at such high speed, and the oil-starved 400 motor could have "thrown a piston," right through the wall of the engine block! - just like in a NASCAR race.

I remained breathless. My armpits soaked: I had to relax. It took a few minutes before my nerves - and heart beat..."lub-dub...lub-dub...lub-dub" - could return to normal.

But to me, It was well worth it! I had totally and completely embarrassed this Mopar hot shot in front of his "companion." (ha -ha) What greater satisfaction exists than that? I could now picture what this embarrassed GTX guy was saying to his hottie girlfriend..."Er; maybe I need a tune up?" Plus it was such an improbable occurrence! Never to be forgotten by me; or this hot-shot GTX driver. What a heart-pounding race it had been! I got back into the GTO - thinking to myself: "You stupid gashole... what if you'd "blown-up" the engine in Mom's gorgeous GTO? What then?

Then I headed for the nearest gas station, to add half a quart.: Gotta keep that oil level at the FULL mark."

Next stop: home. My sweaty armpits were becoming a bit pungent: Time to change into a nice, clean shirt: Nevertheless, the sweet scent of victory "hung in the air."

QUOTE:

"The first shall be last. And the last shall be first."

"Scratch one 440 Plymouth GTX!"

YEAH!

Chapter 20

AUGUST 1969:

It was a late Saturday afternoon: I was HOT IN pursuit of a bronze 69 Z-28 Camaro - chasing him all the way out Market street - trying to line up at a red light: (typical lunatic me)

A 68 Z-28 Camaro

I knew ALL about the Z-28: another "sheep" in wolf's clothing (i.e.) highly overrated. Yet all you'd hear about Z-28s was how fast they were! They were NOT. "Hot Rod Magazine" said QUOTE:

"The Z-28 is a race car dressed up in street clothes."

Baloney. A race car?

No free-keen way! I knew because I was someone with an actual, street-racing "background." Z-28 Camaros sure looked & SOUNDED like race cars; but ran as if their trunks were overloaded with watermelons.

It was that imposing "E-E-E-WHOOOM" (solid-lifter) engine sound that made one think a Z-28 was super fast: but realistically, Z-28s were all sound; but no FURY (i.e.) Paper tigers...a big ROAR- but no BITE.

At Ohio State, my fraternity brother, Mike Meredith (Dayton, OH) drove a red, 68 Z-28. Of course, Mike thought his "Z" was the baddest -fastest, nastiest Camaro around.

We'd go looking for races on Summit Ave: a wide, smooth one way street; absolutely ideal for street racing. One night - after we'd been down Summit for about the 5th time - a studious-looking guy (mid-20s) pulls alongside at a red light - driving a blue 65 327 Corvette...his LADY beside him riding shotgun. He looked over with a "sly" smile on his face: a hint that he might "wanna give it a go." (it was a trick) Light changes. Mike put the hammer down! His tires screeching - WHR-WOOOOM! It was off to the races! Meanwhile, this little blue corvette was deliberately hanging way back behind us - going a "proper" 35 mph.

SUCKERS!

It looked as if we were racing an invisible car!

Such embarrassment! We felt like 2 retarded idiots. Even worse, I could imagine what those 2 gasholes in the 'vette were saying to one another..."Ha-ha. "We sure fooled them"..."hee-hee... yuk-yuk" etc.

But blame it on me. I knew it was all my fault: "PWS" strikes again: I should have warned Dave about "PWS" (i.e.) pussy-whipped syndrome. I was the world's most foremost EXPERT on this enigmatic subject: It went like this:

DEFINITION: PWS - "If a guy driving a hot car is with his chick, its 99% probable he won't be 'shifting his stick.'" (4-SPEED transmission).

Never could I figure out why females HATED street racing (e.g.) "Don't you dare...I'll get MAD if you race him!" (i.e.) "no midnight nooky-wooky for you, bad boy." Do what the lady tells you. Be nice.

Naturally, Meredith thought his Z-28 Camaro was some mean screamin' machine. Nope. His 302 solid lifter Chevy engine sounded nasty. REALLY LOUD. It red-lined at an unbelievable 7000 RPM; but it wasn't FAST.

Under max acceleration, my head did not snap back! Dave's car seemed woefully lacking in torque. Meanwhile, back on Market street - finally - I'd caught up with this 69 Z-28, in the left lane at a red light.

This car was vibrating with an incredibly noisy idle; like being parked next to my Dad's cement mixer - BANGING CLATTERING away. It was those damm solid-lifter valves!

The light went yellow for the intersecting street. I couldn't wait to show this hot-shot my tail lights: Light changes: VROOOOOOOOOM! Mom's GTO easily blew away this Camaro by at least five car lengths. I was laughing - viewing his car way behind me in my mirror.

Pulling up beside me at the next red light, said the astonished Z -driver..."Man, your goat gets outta the hole, FASTER than any other car I've ever seen! You oughta take that thing out to Quaker!"

Then, he drove away.

"Hey...not a bad idea! Take Mom's goat out to the dragstrip and REALLY get some acclamation; perhaps win a trophy!"

NOTE: Quaker City was an NHRA-sanctioned drag strip, about 15 miles west in Salem, Ohio.

Next Sunday, late afternoon - I was heading down Ohio Route 11. Destination: Salem OH (Quaker CITY)... about a 25 minute drive. The time trials started at 6 PM.

CAUTION: I was about to enter "the RADAR ZONE." I was ON ALERT - ever-vigilant for those wonderful, "dedicated" Ohio State troopers- blithely issuing (kah-ching) 75 dollar SPEEDING citations - saving

INNUMERABLE numbers of lives!

These bad boy cops would hide at the bottom of a downhill grade; on a right hand curve. So, whenever a "speeder" rounds the blind curve - GOTCHA - there sat the cop, "taking pictures." But this wasn't candid camera (don't smile): it was a RADAR trap!

Is this REALLY saving lives? Sure. Just keep cranking out all those 75 dollar speeding citations - easy as printing U.S. currency. Of course, these elitist cops ALWAYS maintained that they're doing it for "SAFETY"...because "Speed" kills: But who or what is "SPEED?" Amphetamines? Some intangible, invisible, Orwellian force - that inescapably crashes down upon your car, the instant you exceed the limit?

Think about it: Sure, speed kills; but ONLY if you COLLIDE with someone (or something). Driving on a "limited access highway" (freeway) what is there to COLLIDE with? - other than an occasional deer carcass.

Yeah, the "O-H-P"- the Ohio Highway Patrol: bringing laughter & joy into people's lives everyday. What we would do without them?

But actually, would it not be more pragmatic to call them "O-R-P" (i.e.) the OHIO REVENUE PATROL?

Safety?...GIMME A BREAK! One cop - writing twenty, 75 dollar speeding tickets everyday - equals BIG BUCKS!

20 tickets x75 dollars =$1500 x 365days/yr = 547,500 dollars/year:

REPEAT: from just ONE cop! Ergo, a critical revenue source for the "beloved" state of Ohio. Then, just ahead, I saw a lurid, sinister-looking, plum purple 69 Dart - "all dressed up as a race car," with garish stripes. Hood adornments.

Big, rectangular dual exhausts. The whole works. I was beguiled: this Dart looked insanely out of the ordinary vs. a "plain vanilla" Dodge Dart.

The mystery Dart exited at Rt. 224...5 miles west of Market st. On a whim I followed him, and stopped beside him at the next light. I saw a white racing stripe - encompassing the Dart's rear deck; with a pronounced logo saying..."SWINGER." WTF? Strange name for a car. I always thought swingers were wife swappers.

Then, on the hood, two engine call-outs saying..."340." Hmmm: I'd NEVER heard of any 340 Swinger. I was in for quite the surprise: Looking over at this cocky, arrogant driver (early

20's) - wearing cheap sunglasses- that LOOK of supreme confidence in his face told me this Dart could be BIG-BIG trouble.

Light changes! The Dart flew out of the chute, like an arrow from a bow - putting a 2 car hole-shot on the GTO! Fortunately, I caught him at 70, then eased away.

The 340 lacked top end torque...it's only weakness. But in a EIGHTH mile race, the Dart would've won...easily. Ironically, I thought...."Wow, that 340 Dart gets out of the hole faster than anything I've ever seen."

(six months later)

It was now Spring of 1970. The now-dreaded Chrysler 340 was indeed, another "LITTLE ENGINE THAT COULD."

It had taken the streets by storm. In late summer '69, It had hit the streets un-announced; but went on to raise holy hell at red lights everywhere.

The new molten-hot 340 Mopar engine was called a "disruptor." A "giant killer."

I sure wasn't too keen to race another. If you asked me, they should've re-branded it the "340 SCREAMER." Not surprisingly, Chrysler had the 340 option available in every small model: Duster. Demon. Dart Swinger. Dart GT. Barracuda. AAR Barracuda. Dodge Challenger. Dodge Challenger TA.

A '70 Dodge Challenger

Even the 1970 Roadrunner had the 340 option. My-gawd! 340s were everywhere! So what next? 340 ice cream trucks? A 340 school bus? How 'bout a 340 ambulance? 340 stretch-limousines? A 340 Rolls Royce? (4-speed not available)

During summer 1970, 340 Darts descended upon Market Street - like a plague of locusts - "devouring" everything in their path.

Yeah, it was that smart-azz "look" on these drivers' faces that so unnerved me. They drove the hottest machine on the street; and acted like it. It was hard to believe just how quickly these nasty, nervy, supremely-arrogant hot shots had changed street racing - for the WORSE!

They'd look over at me with a vile facial expression; as if saying..."Suck my exhaust pipe dude; in your piggy GTO!"

Ergo, I would avoid these 340 hot shots by staying on Belmont as much as possible - especially at night. One day on Belmont, I saw another 340: a brown 1970 Plymouth Duster - lining up beside me at a red light.

You should've seen this driver! He sure wasn't no city slicker – looking like Johnny Hilljack, fresh out of the Ozarks. He was clad in buckskin leather - looking as if he were direct descendant of Ma 'n Pa Kettle...born in a log cabin. Perhaps his ancestry had fought at the Alamo. He had some kind of bizarre, leather "watchama-call-it" dangling from his rear view mirror. Probably had a Mossberg "over-under" shotgun under the front seat. I looked over - asking..."wanna race that 340?" Ozark Johnny arrogantly replied..."Not unless you wanna go for FIVE!"

Yeah. A real "businessman" behind the wheel. We ended up NOT racing. He drove off. Next, at Rt 304 and Belmont, I lined up against a fearsome 6 pack yellow 1970 Superbee; with its "trap door" hood (A-12 option).

A '69 Superbee Dodge

These 440 tri-power Dodge Coronets were pure bad-azz- not to be fooled with!

Guy driving (mid -20s, sunglasses) looks over and was ACTUALLY laughing at me - like I was Bozo the Clown! What a smart-alecky SOB! When the light changed, I went screaming away; while this 24-carat bunghole was DELIBERATELY hanging way back in the right lane - doing about 30 mph.

Slowing down, I asked him why he'd dogged out: "Ha-hah-ha...I wouldn't waste my gas on your pig GTO...ha ha ha!' (a really nice guy he was) Afterwards, I thought, "DAMMIT...street racing used to be such a blast."

But no longer: Summer 1969 had HIT THE ROAD.

Now in 1970 - seemingly everywhere - were arrogant, insulting, mean-spirited Mopar drivers - impossible to avoid. They were out in abundance. Sadly, these nasty boys had taken away much of the fun I once had...engaged in my "ultimate sport"- hunting down hot shots in my Mother's GTO.

Chapter 21

JULY: 1969

- QUESTION: Who was it that said… "Ya can't win 'em all." (harrump-harrumph): "Well, I respectfully beg to DIFFER."

- Driving Mom's drop-top GTO was like a fantastic, never-ending journey down Victory Lane! Like watching ABC's "Wide World of Sports," it was indeed THE THRILL of VICTORY!

- Believe it, man; you NEVER get tired of always winning! Ever see any happy losers? In national sporting events, the winners always are celebrated; but the losers? NOPE.

- For example:
    - Vince Lombardi Trophy for the Super Bowl.
    - Run for the Roses at the Kentucky Derby
    - Wearing the Green Jacket in Augusta at the Masters.
    - The winner's circle after the Daytona 500.
    - The Baseball World Series' Commissioner's Trophy
    - Larry O'Brian Trophy of the NBA
    - the Crystal Football for NCAA college championship
    - the Wimbleton Silver Plate trophy

Mom's amazing GTO was UNTIED and UNDEFEATED. I felt untouchable! The light would turn green and it was "Good Night Irene." Imagine the sublime feeling of "ALWAYS WINNING."

But what about those other guys, who lost? (i.e.) Plymouth Roadrunner hot-shots: the sorest losers of them all! Unwilling to accept the truth...that a so-called "pig GTO" had badly whipped 'em all - decisively! (poor lads)

A '69 Plymouth Roadrunner

Roadrunners were like World War 2 Japanese Kamikaze pilots - attacking unremittingly; only to be ignominiously SHOT DOWN in flames.

Kamikaze pilots flew badly-outdated, long-obsolete aircraft. Some could not even exceed 200 mph; easily targeted by US Navy 40 mm. range finders...shot down in multitudes; like clay pigeons (i.e.) target practice. Long live the Emperor! Road Runner drivers did likewise. They were undaunted. Aggressive. DETERMINED - but sorely lacking in firepower; like hunting a grizzly with a Daisy

BB rifle. Sure: Road Runners were quick...but they weren't FAST! Their 335 horse, 383 cube engines seemed woefully under-powered vs. Mom's bad-to-the-bone GTO. (pity)

Interestingly, was how all these drivers all acted so supremely ARROGANT, while waiting at red lights. I'd be laughing. I guess they thought "Roadrunner" IMPLIED that they were driving some really NASTY, bad-azz, fantastic car.

Finally, I figured it out: Mystery solved.

A Roadrunner driver - EVERY time he opened his door - saw the cartoonish "logo" of the zany roadrunner bird - churning through the desert - happily leaving everything in the dust.

Hence - subconsciously (subliminally) roadrunner drivers came to (falsely) believe that they too, could DUST anyone who challenged them!

How could they even THINK 335 horsepower was enough to win on the street with CONSISTENCY? They all acted cocky; like they had something to prove: Some score to settle. A loss to be avenged. Whatever.

In my estimation, the way I'd blow them all away - usually by 4-5 or even six car lengths - they should've called them "Plymouth Roadwalkers." They did NOT run all that fast!

HOWEVER... if a Roadrunner had the HEMI option, it was a DIFFERENT story. You'd be messing with one mighty Mopar.

In 1969, a Plymouth street hemi - with 425 horses - costa plenty: 741 dollars ABOVE sticker price. In today's money it would be equivalent to $7,000: not exactly chump change. So virtually any Roadrunner you'd encounter, had the lame 'n tame 383

Mopar standard engine; a real cream puff! One night on Market street, I spotted a white 69 Roadrunner with Goodyear polyglas tires. The driver was ignoring me altogether. We were side-by-side, at a red light. Thinking it was a 383, I was almost laughing!

Then, on its hood, the engine call-outs said "HEMI." An instantaneous wake up call! I now faced the so-called UNBEATABLE Hemi... the terror of the asphalt jungle!

Suddenly, I felt this huge adrenaline RUSH! A rapid heart beat...incredible suspense!

FLASHBACK: 1964: I was reading a "Sports Illustrated" story; where Chrysler talked about developing a massive "KING KONG" hemi engine for NASCAR race tracks: Daytona and Talladega in particular.

A "King Kong" Hemi engine? Hmmm. I wondered: perhaps Chrysler had made a grievous mistake - branding their new "monster" engine as "King Kong."

Ergo, why not call it the "Godzilla" Hemi engine? YES! After all; everyone knows that Godzilla was much tougher and stronger than King Kong: (no contest).

Finally - on February 27, 1966 - "Kong" emerged from the jungle, in the form of Richard Petty – driving his hemi-powered #43 blue Plymouth - winning the Daytona 500.

It was myth turning reality: Chrysler had hit the jackpot in public relations. Overnight, the HEMI had now entered the national spotlight as this fearsome, 426 cubic inch monster - and you could ride this beast at any local Mopar dealer. Increased foot traffic in Dodge and Plymouth showrooms was duly noted.

A hemi evoked pure raw power under the hood (i.e.) 425 horsepower. In the Chrysler line-up of cars, the Hemi batted clean up. By far, its engine dwarfed all others. Under the hood, sat a gargantuan V8 - topped off by TWO- four barrel Carter carburetors...a towering inferno of horse power!

So here I am, sitting terrified at this red light - completely intimidated. I was about to go head-to- head with an UNBEATABLE hemi!

Lord have mercy!

I was trembling. My confidence - melting rapidly away, like ice cream in summer sunlight. PANIC: should I dog out? Would this be my first time losing?

The hemi driver (mid-20's) was looking straight ahead; with that "all GTOs are pigs" smirk on his face.

To him, it would be like Goliath over David. The '61 Yankees vs the '61 Mets. Ohio State vs. the College of Wooster. Notre Dame vs. the Coast Guard Academy. Secretariat vs. a plow horse. A total blow-out!

Then, before I could even finish saying my prayers, the red light turned green!

Acting "instinctively," I nailed the gas pedal: VAROOOOOOOM! Mom's hypersonic GTO streaked out to a startling HALF car lead...the hemi's headlights even with my door!

Never will I EVER forget those bright headlights- right beside me; only a few feet away. I saw the hemi driver: he was clenching his teeth! Everything seemed to be running in slow motion. A brief time warp of intensive drama. Thundering sounds from his two, four barrel carbs - were indescribable: My eardrums were begging for mercy!

"WAH- WOOOOOOOM." With 425 horses beneath his hood, I kept waiting for him to pull away. But no!

Miraculously, a mere 10 feet behind me- the howling, roaring roadrunner could NOT make up the shortfall - staying even with my door to the next red light.

A "race to end all races"... and I WON!"

I was breathless: the biggest, baddest Mopar on the street - going down to defeat!

I sat relieved behind the wheel. My armpits were soaked.

From terror to ecstasy in less than a minute!

I felt like the war hero who had charged an enemy machine gun- and SURVIVED.

Thank the Lord above...If I'd lost, this high 'n mighty hemi driver would have been laughing like a hyena... "ALL GOATS ARE PIGS."

Panic had descended upon him - defeated by a "pig" GTO. To him, something virtually impossible.

Alarms were going off in his head! The look on his face. It all added up - undoubtedly the FIRST time he'd ever lost a street race!

Waiting at the next red light, he looked so infuriated, I thought he was about to experience an aneurysm! (call 9-1-1) In complete frustration, he yelled over: "THAT GOAT AIN'T STOCK!" "Pull over...I'll show you the engine." Hood open - after looking underneath - he seemed completely flabbergasted: a total loss for words. Using perfect timing, I decided to give this yo-yo my verbal coup de gras "See; it's a stock 400/350...it's not even my car...this is my Mother's GTO."!

Driving away, he looked totally bewildered - a shocking wake-up call!

His worst nightmare come true - losing to a lowly GTO.

Indeed, for a long time thereafter, he would suffer from "PTGD" (i.e.) Post Traumatic Goat DISORDER - a night he'd never forget.

And for me? Permanent bragging rights: Something "I could tell to my grandchildren."

In summation: a famous football coach had said it best: QUOTE:

"Winning isn't everything...it's the only thing." Vince Lombardi: Packers' 1959 summer training camp.

Chapter 22

A '68 Charger RT

JULY - 1969:

It was Friday afternoon:

I was working for Dad - hauling bricks and cement for his brick-laying crew. The brick work was nearing completion: Of course, Dad wanted THIS job finished today; so the NEXT job could begin early Monday morning... 8 AM. (efficiency)

Dad - always the businessman - promised a bonus to the bricklayers... IF the work "could be done today."

But working overtime on FRIDAY? Oh-my-god!

Dad's work crew always would get "itchy" on Fridays – eager to skedaddle and go cash their paychecks; as soon as it was quitting time (4:30 pm).

And so, after the bricklayers had ceased with all their gnashing of teeth and murmuring- the 'verdict' was in...'NO WORKING past "quittin' time."

Ergo, they'd leave at 4:30 pm...so their wives "wouldn't be worried."

Dad looked at me..."Mix up a double (load of cement) Ricky... we'll have this job finished before dark!" 8 PM. Dad and I were pulling into the driveway (home).

PROBLEM: my sister had bitterly out-fought me, over..."who was next in the bathroom." Hence, I eventually got out to Market street late - after 10 pm. "Oh what a night!" It was perfect convertible weather! Mom's gorgeous, drop-top GTO - 8 track blasting - seemed like a dreamy, "magic carpet ride" up Market street on this Friday evening. Soon, I was behind a nasty-sounding, black 68 440 Charger RT; with its huge, rectangular (cow bell) dual exhausts - rumbling ominously.

By summer 1969, Dodge Charger RTs - with that nasty, 440 Super Commando V8 under their hoods - had well-established they were the "kings of the road." Practically unbeatable from any red light.

Nonetheless, it was an ideal time to show this bad-boy RT jockey "who's the boss." I had soundly-whipped a 69 440 GTX Plymouth a week before on the I-680 freeway. We were both lined-up at a red light: Glancing over at this arrogant RT driver (about 20) he was trying to conceal his laughter! I could read his aloof facial expression..."HAH! Another jerk driving a pig GTO... hardy har!" Then, the red light changed to green:

"VRROOOOOM" - It was like "Gone With the Wind." Mom's GTO blew away this RT hot shot so decisively, that he probably went home! (i.e.) "Hit the road, JACK!"

QUOTE:

"He who laughs last...laughs best."

Then, on impulse, I headed for Belmont ave. I had a "mission" to fulfill: A greaser at the Clark gas station had told me that Joey Dellafiore - in his red 68 L-78 Chevelle - "was looking for me"- planning to blow me away. It was the fastest car in Girard; a nearby small town.

Hence, I began a search for yet another L-78 hot shot, who thought his SS Chevelle was unbeatable. (L-78 option- 375 horsepower).

QUOTE:

"He who exalts himself, shall be humbled."

It was almost midnight. I knew I had to find this L-78 before it got too late. "Time was of the essence."

Hence, I was ready to pray to the Almighty Lord Himself:

QUOTE:

"Seek; and ye shall find... Knock, and it shall be opened."

Glancing at the gas gauge, it fluttered on "E." Low on "petrol." A 24-hr. Sunoco was the only station open late on Belmont.They were out of premium; however, they did have Sunoco 260 "super premium" on the "custom blending" pump. At 44.9/gallon, it was 15 cents above Shell conventional premium (i.e.) "Ethyl."

WOW! Surprise-surprise! Pulling back onto Belmont..."SCREEEECH"- the back tires broke loose! My head snapped back! Instantly Mom's goat seemed as if powered by rocket fuel! An amazing boost in torque!

"EUREKA!"...I felt like "Archimedes" - emerging triumphantly from his bath tub. I'd discovered - quite by happenstance - a POTENT new weapon (260 gasoline) to employ in the street wars around town! YES!

Heading north - 8 track tape player blasting- I was praying that a red 68 SS Chevelle might miraculously appear. Pulling into Arby's, the parking

lot wasn't even half full: Nope; no red 68 SS Chevelle. I was about to give up all hope. Dang it! I wanted to find this L-78 hotshot in the worst possible way. Then, BINGO! I saw a gorgeous, black, 69 Dodge Charger RT – two aboard - waiting at the Route 304 red light.

Wow; thank you DEAR LORD! Another race with a 440 RT Charger! Two for the price of ONE!

But something didn't add up: The two in the RT paid no attention at all to me, as I pulled alongside. Plus; they kept their radio blasting away. Sure fooled me.

Then, a nasty SURPRISE: this crafty RT driver "jump-started" me – hitting the gas "prematurely"- just BEFORE the green light.

The fast-accelerating RT Charger went streaking away...."B-R-R-R-A--WHOOOOOOOOOM.'

Angered, I floored the GTO... hot in pursuit of the black Dodge; at least 5-6 car-lengths down the road...."VAR-OOOOOOOOOM."

Wow! Mom's goat screamed forward - as if turbo charged! I had the "hammer down!"

I was gaining on them! It was like FLYING! I became George Jetson...I caught them at 80 mph!

The astonished RT driver took his foot off the gas - motioning me to pull over. Parked roadside, he jogged up to me..." Wow, I never saw a GTO that could STAY with me like that."

ME: "WHAT? STAY with you? I was about to pass you up!"

Let's race again." He agreed.

This RT driver had seen me closing rapidly in his mirror. So why was he so willing to race again? Of course! He couldn't fathom losing to some "pig" GTO. Time to give these two gasholes a great view of my tail lights.

I played starter: "OK... we'll go from a ten roll: one... two... THREE!"

Whoom! Mom's GTO literally ROCKETED ahead - powered by the "rocket fuel" 260 gasoline.

Bye-bye... I began pulling away! I was in stitches! LMAO.

After the RT drove up to me; these two jokers looked totally freaked-out; as if awakened from a nightmare. "Hey man... what's in that goat? Is it ram air?"

"Nope - 400/350...COMPLETELY stock."

"No way! Can you pull over and pop the hood?"

The GTO's hood open, they began a deliberate, thorough inspection – like customs officers searching for contraband - finding nothing.

Triumphantly, I said: "See? No ram air! It's not even my car... this is my Mother's GTO."

AFTERMATH: Driving home, I never felt so darn PROUD in my entire life! Mom's GTO had literally ANNIHILATED two fearsome Charger 440 RTs in one night!

Being a World War 2 enthusiast, I thought of a historical parallel; the greatest naval engagement of the war: when Germany's "unsinkable" Bismarck ANNIHILATED the British capital ship -HMS Hood - literally BLOWING it out of the water after just 10 minutes of battle!

The Bismarck – A mighty German Battleship

Since the Germans had state-of-the-art, optical range-finders coupled to the Bismarck's massive, 15-inch guns, they had the Hood "zeroed-in" (bracketed) after the second volley.

Imagine: the Bismarck could place a devastating 15-inch shell "right on the money" from 30,000 yards (17 nautical miles). Some mighty good shootin' I would opine - considering that Hood was maneuvering and turning: British Admiral Lance Holland – taking evasive action as best as he knew how.

But just when the Bismarck fired off its third volley, Admiral Holland zigged, when he should've "zagged"...KA-BOOOOOOM; a direct hit in the Hood's main powder magazine!

The good admiral - along with 1,503 Hood sailors - "bought the farm." (i.e.) the government death benefit - paid out to each sailor's surviving widow - would pay off the farm's outstanding mortgage.

Suddenly, I realized that with a half-tank of high-octane Sunoco 260, Mom's GTO - much like the mighty Bismarck - would really be "unsinkable" (unbeatable)!

ANTICIPATION: I couldn't wait to hit Market street again, and blow "em all right outta the water"... in Mom's devastating 69 GTO!

"AHOY...FULL SPEED AHEAD."

"Aye-aye, sir."

Chapter 23

AUGUST - 1969:

IT WAS A FRIDAY AFTERNOON:

I was driving on Market street - riding with the top down - looking around: Ah, what a pleasant sight! The color of GREEN! (money) Youngstown was flush with bucks! WORKING People driving new cars... going on vacations...making down payments on new homes, etc.

LET THE GOOD TIMES ROLL!

Youngstown WAS literally boom town USA - money flowing through the city in a bountiful abundance!

It was because of increasing WORLDWIDE demand for American steel. And

high-quality Youngstown steel was some of the best made ANYWHERE.

Being third in worldwide steel production; with its 55,000 union steel jobs – Youngstown had the highest median income of any U.S. mid-size clty back in the 60s.

On Friday night, banks would be open till 8 PM - cashing the hefty paychecks of WORKING people- waiting in line to collect their hard-earned loot.

Suddenly, it hit me - thinking...”it just doesn't get ANY BETTER than this.” Sitting behind the wheel of Mom's gorgeous 69 GTO convertible, - eight track blasting- I felt most fortunate to be experiencing this urban utopia.

"Thank you dear Lord!"

In steel, Youngstown ranked THIRD world wide, in gross tonnage produced. However, in the 60's, Market street was FIRST - an INCREDIBLE place to street race - primarily because of the cops; or lack thereof. Since Youngstown had a bountiful municipal tax base (i.e.) steel mills; Youngstown cops could truly act as POLICE - caring little about traffic tickets.

The Youngstown Police were about reducing crime; and nothing else. Now imagine this: YOU have just been stopped by some sneaky traffic cop - after hiding somewhere with his DEADLY radar gun.

COP: "Sorry sir...I got you clocked going 44 in a 35 zone. I'll have to issue you a ticket."

YOU: "What? A TICKET? Why aren't you cops out catching the real CRIMINALS?"

But then a miracle:

COP: "You're absolutely right sir. God, what was I thinking? There's this nine year old cold murder case that I've been meaning to look into."

Back to reality: Today's punk arrogant traffic cops, seldom - if ever – will issue a warning.

So now, that flimsy, pink (or blue) 145-dollar speeding ticket you're holding in your hand, not only ruins your day; but probably your week, month - even LONGER.

You have options (choices) all of them BAD!

- mail in the paid ticket: 145 of your hard earned dollars, down the drain.

- call grandma, to "borrow" 145 dollars - call a traffic attorney, to plead down to a "non-moving" violation

- call the traffic court: you need to change your appearance date

- call work: you'll be in court on a certain day Several weeks later, you receive a "WE NOTICED" letter: "Dear policy holder: 'We noticed' a recent moving violation on your driver's license report. Therefore, your new monthly premium will rise from 77/month, to 119/month.

Thank You For Choosing Geico."

Now let's add it all up: 145 for ticket. 42 dollar monthly increase in insurance 42 x 12 = 404 annual increase...extrapolated out ten years: 404 x 10 years = 4,040 DOLLARS! Gone! ALL because demon you "broke the LAW!"

Now you're well underway to becoming a hardened CRIMINAL.

Perhaps a guidance counselor might be of some help; or seek out your local clergy.

Tell you what BRO; if this sounds like you, you should be in Youngstown.

If one went through a 4 way stop; or doing 45 in a 35, a Youngstown cop would "let you slide."

But if you called the cops about someone kicking down your door — or robbing a store - they'd literally be there in TWO minutes. They had their priorities right...STOPPING the BAD GUYS.

Speeding tickets in Youngstown? Radar traps? Rare. Practically non-existent. And if you "knew" someone, any issued ticket could be "fixed." I remembered a while back: I was in a hurry - going down Mahoning Ave (west side); when - zippity-do-dah - I crashed a red light. No big deal. This was an "unnecessary red light." Brilliant move. I had not bothered to look at my mirror; and now it displayed a Youngtown POLICE cruiser - lights flashing - pulling me over to STOP.

COP: "Do you know why I stopped you?"

ME: "Yeah."

COP: "Let's see your license." (glanced at it for about 30 seconds)

COP: "Do you still live on the north side?"

ME: "Yeah!"

COP: "Is Jimmy your brother?"

ME: "Yeah!"

COP: "You can go."

Now, compare this to a Cleveland traffic stop...which

I experienced a long time ago:

SETTING: Cleveland Ohio. Lost on some dark freeway:

I decided to get off at the next exit. Bad move.

I found myself driving through what looked like Eastern Botswana.

It was roll up windows - lock all doors - territory:

The street could've been named '"CAR JACK AVE."

And straight ahead, was the proverbial "unnecessary" red light.

To crash? Or not to crash? I decided on option one- crash this stupid light.

Bad move: INSTANTLY, a sneaky, hidden Cleveland cop pulled me over.

COP: "Let me see your license."

ME: "C'mon officer. There's no reason for that light to be working this late."

COP: "IF you continue to argue, I'll call for a back-up."

What a humiliating, maddening experience! Eventually, I had to cough-up 165 dollars; for a "failure to obey a traffic signal."

And then a 'stop sign' incident - occurring in a little town, just across the Youngstown border. I was going through the center of town; when - going about 3 mph - I rolled through the 4-way stop.

Bad move:

Instantly, this small town cop - hiding in a parking lot - pulls out with lights flashing; and proceeds to pull me over.

COP: "Do you know why you were stopped?"

ME: "I have no idea."

COP: "You failed to come to a COMPLETE STOP! You could've RUN OVER a little kid!"

ME: "That's right officer...I almost ran over an INVISIBLE little kid."

Bad move:

Instantly, this punk cop does an about face; and - after 10 minutes in his car - hands me TWO tickets. A 75 dollar "seat belt violation" and a 150 dollar "failure to stop."

Unbelievable! 225 bucks; just for smarting-off to some anal, small town cop!

And what about that universal mantra? - put forth by the so-called "Establishment."

"SPEED KILLS."

Sure, speed kills; BUT only if you COLLIDE with something (or someone).

Think about it: -Ridiculously low speed limits; on freeways designed for 80 mph - 4-way stop signs EVERYWHERE, on less-traveled side streets; with a cop hiding nearby - 24 hour red lights- at intersections bereft of ANY crossing traffic.

It's all about "SAVING LIVES"- right?

Nope.

It's all about DELIBERATELY creating DISRESPECT for the LAW!

What if all those unnecessary red lights...unnecessary 4-way stops, were removed?

What if all the ridiculously low speed limits were raised by 10 or 15 mph? What would happen? Carnage on the streets, and highways? Nope. Nothing would happen. They're there to antagonize the driving public. Hence, drivers eventually come to ignore absurd traffic stop signs and lowball speed limits.

Result: EVENTUALLY, they ALL end up with a high dollar traffic ticket!

And where does all that money go? To municipal traffic courts - requiring an "infrastructure" of judges...bailiffs...sheriffs...clerical workers...traffic lawyers, etc.

Even worse. You must pay with CASH; which cannot easily be traced. Such a fantastic way to "create" new jobs! PERMANENT jobs!

But all sarcasm aside fellow citizens: Aren't these judicial/law enforcement types getting what is essentially a FREE ride? - living off our "misfortune" (i.e.) traffic tickets.

No. I am NOT advocating we eliminate courts, judges, traffic cops, tickets, support people, etc. That would be ANARCHY.

All I wanna know is why in the world these "whopper" traffic fines costa so MUCH?

Even worse, they tack on COURT COSTS. Which of course begs the question... how much should a court COST? How much should a so called "magistrate" be paid, for telling a guilty driver..."You can plead NO contest."

And what happens if you DO plead NO contest? Does this mean you can NEVER AGAIN enter a Publisher's Clearing House contest?

But wait; there's MORE!

WHAT about all those PREDATORY Auto insurance companies? - sucking the lifeblood out of our checking accounts. Indeed - in their insipid TV commercials - do they not portray themselves as good-natured problem solvers?- trying to keep your insurance rates as LOW as possible. When, in reality, they've managed to bullshift the driving public (i.e.) "You gotta SPEEDING ticket." Ergo, you must PAY heavily for this "egregious offence" (i.e.) "SHOW US THE MONEY; you reckless driver!"

Now consider this old, well-worn proverb: "What goes up; must come down."

But NOT for auto insurance rates! Never-ever does the insured get a letter:

"Dear policy-holder:

We are happy to inform you - because of your clean driving record - that we are lowering your monthly insurance premium"...etc.

Indeed; receiving such a letter is as likely as a snowstorm in the Sahara. Once again; let's add it up over 10 years - using a 19 dollar/month hypothetical rate hike:

12 x 19 dollars = 228 (annual rate hike)

10 x 228 = 2,280 DOLLARS over 10 years!

Hard-earned MONEY; out of YOUR pocket.

A sum that would've enabled you to put a down payment on a HOUSE. Or buying new furniture. Eating filet mignon vs. fried baloney. Shopping at Bloomingdales vs. K-mart.

Even worse; there is no reasonable alternative (i.e.) FORCED ACCEPTANCE: take it or leave it. Like it or lump it.

CAUTION: if one dare go without auto insurance - WHAM! Eventually you will lose your license. Auto insurance is mandatory in the "lower 48."

Sad to say, fellow drivers:These rapacious auto insurance companies have – under our collective noses - surreptitiously evolved into a CARTEL...the auto insurance CARTEL!

Indeed, like OPEC, do they not all work in concert?- keeping rates artificially HIGH!

But what should we do, fellow citizens? What can be done to fight back? Very little. Actually, nothing can be done to "fight back."

Sadly, the "Establishment" knows that the "average Joe driver" is just too damm busy with life. Too busy out earning a living- leaving little time for much else.

To the Establishment, we're all just insignificant, dinky little cogs - turning within a gigantic, societal wheel.

It's just like that old 80s Pink Floyd song:

"All in all - you're just another brick in the wall."

'Drive safely.'

Chapter 24

SUNDAY: JULY 20, 1969

America was breathlessly awaiting the Apollo moon landing; scheduled for around 11 pm.

The whole world would be watching...including yours truly.

To me, this event stood equal to America's completion of the Transcontinental Railroad - May 10, 1869 - exactly a century before.

Ever since my elementary school days, I found American history so incredibly fascinating. It was if America had been DESTINED for greatness.

1781: General George Washington, AGAINST all odds - defeated the odious British at Yorktown - thereby ending the 5 year Revolutionary War.

Such a grand and noble way to inaugurate our beloved country!

Then, during the War of 1812, the country's inspirational national anthem came to the forefront: "The land of the free; and the home of the brave."

Wow. What other country could be described in such a positive light? NONE.

America survived a civil war.

American soldiers were germane in ending the First World War. America won World War 2 - rescuing the world from fascism (Hitler) and fanaticism (Japan). Post-war, America saved Europe from the evil progression of communism. (Marshall Plan) By the middle of the 20th century, America stood out for its goodness...its generosity. Its benevolence.

FLASHBACK- January, 1961: I remember watching President John Kennedy - making his historic inaugural address..."Ask NOT what your country can do for you" etc.

To me, Kennedy was the very essence of being American:

He was a World War 2 hero. He was brilliant in the execution of his foreign and domestic policies. He prevented a possible THIRD world war (Cuban missile crisis).

Movie star handsome, Kennedy was the "President from central casting."

He was a riveting, inspirational orator. An "aura" of dignity seemed to surround him.

Best of all, it was Kennedy who initiated America's space race to the moon!

FLASHBACK- October, 1957: I was in 3rd grade: I remember coming home from school. Mom was in her bedroom, watching NEWS, rather than her insipid afternoon soap operas.

INSTANTLY, I knew something HUGELY important had occurred:

It was shocking: Russia had put a satellite (Sputnik) in orbit! The effect on America was cataclysmic!

Russia was now AHEAD of the United States in space! INCONCEIVABLE!

The paper boy delivered the newspaper: I read about "Sputnik." I thought it to be a really catchy name - sounding so eminently "Russian."

Near-panic had descended upon the U.S. The "blame game" began. How did the Soviet Union manage to leapfrog the United States in space?

Was NASA asleep at the switch? Explanations were demanded. But none were forthcoming. The US had been caught flat-footed. Such embarrassment - a deep wound in America's national pride.

Even more shocking: Russia's capability to put a MAN in orbit around the Earth; while the US had been struggling to put a mere SATELLITE in orbit.

In 1960, the Soviets succeeded in launching the FIRST man into space (i.e) Yuri Gagarin.

I had to admit: as much as I deeply despised anything Russian; not only had they matched the US in nuclear armaments, they'd clandestinely managed to outpace America in space exploration.

Even Soviet terminology sounded more "advanced:"

The US had ASTRONAUTS.

But the Russians had COSMONAUTS: not only were they ahead in space, they were ahead in nomenclature!

"Cosmonaut" sounded so much more relevant; so much more sophisticated, compared to "Astronaut."

Not surprisingly, by 1961, the space race vs. the Soviet Union had become a national obsession: Americans became preoccupied with NASA. Astronauts. Apollo. Gemini. Rocket engines. Space capsules. Gravitational pull. Orbits. Heat shields: (etc)

Individual NASA astronauts were celebrities- becoming America's newest "rock stars."

Then came the BREAKTHROUGH in May, 1961.

SETTING: Junior High school: 5th period religion class.

Father McCarthy interrupted his lecture to read an important note from the principal's office:

"The United States has succeeded in putting astronaut Alan Shepard into orbit."

It was electrifying! It was instantaneous!

Everyone in class jumped up from their desks -cheering loudly and gesturing wildly! I was elated! Everyone was elated!

Even the dullard Norman Hinchcliff - who sat behind me - was excited. He actually had tears of joy running down his cheeks!

Alan Shepard was now a national hero - appearing on the "Ed Sullivan Show" the following Sunday night.

I was 14 years old. Never will I forget that spontaneous, joyous classroom celebration. Everyone felt so proud to be AMERICAN. Everyone beaming with national pride!

Feeling patriotic was such a happy, positive emotion - displaying the Stars 'n Stripes! Americans everywhere felt UNITED. We'd achieved our common goal - catching-up to the evil, diabolical, HATED Soviet Union. Sadly, that May day in 1961 would prove to be the "high water" mark for America's patriotic fervor in the 20th century. Soon it would go "downhill."

After President Kennedy was gunned down, so began the unbinding of our nation. Inevitably, our national pride slowly bled away, in a wave of recriminations.

WHO would want to shoot John Kennedy? - our beloved and wonderful 34th President.

By 1962, a tidal wave of wealth and prosperity was sweeping over America. People were happy - carrying pocketful's of cash.

Unemployment below 2%. Fortune 500 companies were poaching one another for skilled workers. Dad hired 2 new bricklayers. Calls from new customers began streaming in.

Everyone was thrilled with President Kennedy's tenure in the White House. His approval RATING touched 90%.

Ergo...who would want to kill the goose that laid golden eggs? It would be like conspiring to kill Mother Teresa; who'd done nothing but good works all her life.

Lee Harvey Oswald - who's mother in law was a valued employee at Texas Book Depository - had just started his NEW JOB there, in late October, 1963.

Aiming down through a rifle scope from the 6th floor - 200 feet to the street- it was near-impossible to miss: the easiest sniper shot one could imagine.

But this just did NOT fit it with the gruesome, bloody story line: Therefore, contrive a CONSPIRACY: People wanted ANSWERS. So why not fabricate them? Who would know otherwise? Fame and fortune would quickly follow.

Say it was "a man firing from a sewer." Preposterous. No escape pathway; only a rodent can navigate a contorted municipal sewer network.

Or say it was a rifleman on a "grassy knoll." Even more preposterous! Forty thousand potential witnesses; yet no one saw a determined rifleman - firing from the prone position?

Or pretend to be a ballistics expert - asking how a single (magic) bullet could shatter Kennedy's skull; then careen around the car's interior - finally coming to rest in the wrist of the front passenger Texas governor John Conally.

NOTE: a 30.06 caliber rifle - with a muzzle velocity of 2800 feet/second - can penetrate 3-4 humans if they're standing directly behind one another.

Nevertheless, Americans wanted to know who REALLY was behind it all.

Most certainly, a crime of such magnitude required months - maybe years - of precise planning - implying Fidel Castro; the CIA; or Mafia.

Oswald? No way! A LONE assassin? Impossible!

"Had to be someone acting in concert."

POINT: How could these so-called "conspirators" have done ANY in-depth, long term planning? Kennedy FIRST discussed his plan to visit Dallas with Texas governor John Connally in a phone call on October 4, 1963. (gotcha)

POINT: Lets say these all knowing conspirators did have advanced knowledge of Kennedy's itenerary - Dealy Plaza. Why was the Book Depository - floor 6 - specifically designed a the "ideal spot". This was a highy traveled commercial area. There were hundreds of sites to fire upon the motocade; yet they chose this particular one? **(GOTCHA)**

POINT: the weapon used to shoot Kennedy was a chintzy, Italian-made mail-order hunting rifle. Would not conspirators have chosen a more sophisticated and more accurate weapon; such as the M-14: or a US Army standard-issue sniper rifle? **(GOTCHA)**

POINT: If Oswald was NOT the perpetrator, then WHY did he flee his workplace; then gun down J.D. Tippet, a Dallas police patrolman, in cold blood; then attempt to conceal himself in a movie theater? **(GOTCHA)**

POINT: The first shot struck Kennedy at 12:30 PM Central Standard Time, which correlated exactly with employee lunch period at the Texas Book Depository.

Oswald's job was carting books all day on the lower floors; then, on November 22, rather the employee break room, he decided to "take lunch" on the 6th floor, where out-of-print texts were stored.

MOTIVE: Ideological: Oswald - was a fanatical Marxist and Communist: and so, by definition - he despised ANYTHING American.

Oswald wasn't aiming at Kennedy: To him, he was aiming at the prevailing AMERICAN president - no matter WHO he was at that time: (i.e.) nothing personal - just business. Indeed, America is not a perfect country; but does it not remain the best country in which to live? If you're American, AT LEAST be grateful for your individual liberty. Take not your freedom of speech for granted.

Be thankful that you were fortunate enough to be born in the USA. Be grateful that America's Constitution guarantees our individual liberties (i.e.) the pursuit of happiness.

EXAMPLE #1: let's hypothesize: let's say you called a political talk show to "vent' - saying vitriolically..."I think President Biden is a stupid mother-hugger; and NOT worthy of a second term!"

After hanging up, you feel better...you've gotten it "off your chest."

But where else can you diss a national leader, and get off scott free? What if you lived in ANY other country? What If you lived in Mexico. Vietnam. Columbia. Uganda. Burma. Chile. Bolivia. Botswana. Philippines. Cambodia. Namibia. India...etc

Within 24 hours (or less) there would be an ominous knock on your door (play "Dragnet" theme) and the "secret police" tell you..."please come with us."

EXAMPLE #2: June 2009: Iranian citizens were demonstrating en masse: The streets of Tehran- jammed with tens of thousands of protesters - demanding "western style" freedoms. The repression from the Mullahs they could tolerate no longer.

For a while, the "good guys" (protesters) were winning.

Then the gruesome, bloody response: Ayatollah Ali Khomenei - using Kawasaki motorcycles - dispatched Basij (secret police) to attack individual protesters, demonstrating in the streets. Two aboard, the cycle driver- weaving through the mob of protesters - RANDOMLY singles out the next hapless victim - pulling up from behind; while his rear passenger - POINT-BLANK range - shoots them "cleanly" in the back of the head.

RESULT? the mobs melt away within 48 hours. No one wants to be NEXT.

In the USA such barbarism is unfathomable. Why? Because America is a country that values life.

But for a power-crazed mullah (or dictator) - slaughtering thousands of his own people is (ho-hum) "just another day at the office."

Once again, America- land of the free - remains one of few countries where you can speak your mind freely; without fear of recrimination.

We Americans must learn to appreciate the liberties we enjoy, because they might not be around forever.

(Back to July 20th, 1969)

8:30 pm: Patiently, I'd been waiting two hours for the actual moon landing.

But my patience was wearing thin. It was if someone had punched the "slo- mo" button." The so-called excitement of the impending lunar landing had become ridiculously boring.

The annoying intermittent static- along with the garbled NASA radio transmissions- had become maddening.

Even worse: the dialog seemed jibberish - actually stupid: (e.g.)... "Mission Control...Roger Houston...Roger...Copy...Copy that...Roger...Wilco...Roger Wilco...over and out."

To me, it was a lot of inarticulate babble...particularly "Wilco."

Wilco? What could that POSSIBLY stand for? I had no idea.

I knew of a regional chain of discount stores named "Woolco." These were "big- box" stores serving central Ohio & Columbus.

But "Wilco"? How weird! It sounded like some concoction to plug leaks in a car's radiator (i.e) "Got a leaky radiator? - get WILCO."

Thoroughly bored, I decided that some stop light excitement would be in order (i.e.) DRAG racing! (yeah)

Impulsively, I decided to take Mom's GTO out Market St.

Bad idea:

Market was near deserted; as if hit by a neutron bomb.

Few wanted to miss the lunar landing; but it was still at least two hours way.

Nevertheless, I decided to keep cruising - hoping to race ANYONE who might come along.

Traffic was sparse; but then, a most welcome surprise! Here comes some joker - driving an ugly, dark blue 1965 390 Mercury Marauder- actually trying to RACE ME!

Maurauder Man (about 30) certainly was trying to get my attention. He kept staring over - gunning his engine. Born an intuitive "face reader" I had him pegged immediately: Single - blissfully living at home with mom 'n dad...looking a bit "challenged." (i.e.) mild retard: So no chance whatsoever of him being gainfully employed.

Judging from his eagerness, I sensed he was out for his once- a- week Sunday "joy ride."

Lined up at the red light, Marauder man seemed primed - ready to race - staring directly at me.

Then, it struck me...this guy's just like me! A "kindred spirit"

Only a HARD CORE street racing addict (like me) would be looking for a race on Market street; with cars being so few and far between.

Once an Eagle scout, I'd decided to do my "good turn" for the day. I'd play pretend: allow him to win in the inevitable street race that was about to occur.

Beating a GTO? Wow! This would be his dream come true!

Upon green - "SCREEEEEEECH" - Marauder Man goes zooming away... his right tire leaving a noticeable "strip" on the pavement; while I eased back- giving the GTO "half" throttle - lagging at least 5 cars behind.

Sure enough - at the next red light -

Maurader man had watery eyes - literally overcome with JOY! Waving & flashing me a "thumb's up."

God was he happy! Not only did I "make his day," I might have made his life! - remembering always that July 20, Sunday; when Daddy's 390 Marauder beat a new 69 GTO, with HIM behind the wheel. After that, I decided to give up and head home. I was driving toward downtown, about 2 red lights away from the Market street bridge. Then- music blaring - a MASSIVE, faded blue, 4-door 64 Buick Electra 225 pulls alongside - fully occupied by six young males "of color." I could plainly hear "25 MILES FROM HOME" by Edwin Starr.

They did not appear too friendly. I sensed hostility. Not wanting to make eye contact, I looked straight ahead.

Then, they turned down the volume:

The "youth" riding shotgun, decided to "break the ice."

"Hey white boy... your GTO ain't worth a F**k."

Thinking fast, I quickly retorted...."Yeah, but it's better than your ugly N****R wagon."

Fortunately the red light was changing, as I went zooming away!

Glancing in my mirror, I saw - tumbling end over end - a green Thunderbird bottle - crashing on the pavement in my wake.

The chase was on! Who were they kidding? Did this car full of brothers in a 2-ton Electra - ACTUALLY believe they could catch a GTO?

BRING 'EM ON!

After zooming away, I went flying down Market: then I got a brainstorm! Why not let 'em chase me on the freeway? – knowing they'd never catch up to Mom's strato-jet GTO! Yeah, I'd have a bit of fun with these "road scholars."

Turning left, onto the nearby I-680 freeway ramp, I jammed on the gas: GRRR-ROOOOOOM!

Looking at my rearview mirror, I wondered if they'd taken the "bait."

YES! The massive blue Electra 225 was "hot" in pursuit.

What a laugh!

HOW they EVER expected to catch up to me defied explanation. But this brazen white boy had insulted their beloved monster Buick; so there would be HELL to pay!

Being Sunday night, freeway traffic was light. Ideal for a high-speed chase.

What enfolded next was like a scene adapted from a zany Looney Tunes cartoon: Sylvester is chasing Tweety bird; but just before the cat encloses his grip on little Tweety - he (she?) jumps UP and scoots merrily away!

Likewise; I would speed ahead of my pursuers; then take my foot off the gas – waiting for their "Electra 225" to get about 50 feet behind - then suddenly I'd pull away! (ha-ha)

Whenever I let them get close, the exasperated driver would RAPIDLY flash his bright lights at me. What a genius! Such brilliance!

Were these bad boys actually expecting me to pull over for a cordial, roadside chat?

Looking at them in my mirror; I could easily imagine the "congenial" discussion among them: "C'mon...Hurry up! Catch that *#**#@!%##**#* and run his white azz off the road!"

For about 15 minutes, they continued chasing me: I was in STITCHES! (ROTFLMAO)

Would they ever catch on?

But abruptly, they got off at the next exit (probably low on gas).

Nice try, "soul brothers."

It was after 10 PM. Driving home, I'd decided I'd made a most noble contribution to race relations in America:

All men may have been created equal:

But not all CARS.

MISSION ACCOMPLISHED!

"Roger, Wilco: Over and out."

Chapter 25

AUGUST 1969:

It was around 8 PM: Driving Mom's awesome 69 GTO, I was all psyched-up for another jammin' Friday night on Market street!

"READY-or-NOT... here I COME."

Indeed, Market street was prospering on this hot summer night: People - having cashed their paychecks - were looking to spend their money...(kah-ching). The bars had long lines outside. Traffic heavy. Everyone looking happy- having pocketful's of 20-dollar bills!

I was blasting the 8-track on max volume: Singing MERRILY along:

Not a care in the whole darn world! Mom's GTO was all shined up.

Just then, I heard ominous, thundering booming noises - sounding much like an approaching storm; and the GTO's convertible top was DOWN.

Looking up, I could clearly see the cup 'n handle of the "Big Dipper." So no rain threat tonight.

Obviously, the booming sounds were NOT an approaching thunderstorm. Rather it was the clamor from a marina blue, '66 427 Corvette convertible; with huge-diameter, side exhausts pipes - literally booming like thunder- pulling alongside me in the left lane. You should've seen the driver! Hercules in a tight golf shirt! But this was certainly no golfer: Actually, he looked like he could be play "D -line" for the Oakland Raiders: (i.e.) MASSIVE chest & shoulders. Tall, lanky physique. Sinewy neck. Biceps like stove pipes.

Wearing a well-groomed "goatee"- he looked to be the very epitome of some bad-azz MACHO MAN.

Riding shotgun was his hottie girlfriend - nose arched high in the air - wearing her dark sunglasses.

Rolling alongside me, from light-to-light, Hercules was going to great effort to keep his booming right exhaust pipe EVEN with my driver door; a malevolent "smile" on his face.

DARN! So darn loud! My eardrums were vibrating!

Then it hit me: Hercules was playing with me... like a cat plays with a mouse.

Undoubtedly, Herc probably did this to INTIMIDATE every muscle car driver he might encounter. Result? The driver is quaking in fear, idling next to him at a red light.

Psychological strategy was indeed an inherent part of street racing. "Winning through intimidation" was obviously Herc's game; and he played it masterfully.

His hottie girlfriend seemed to be part of the "act." She was really "yukking it up" as the corvette rolled alongside me.

But if the villainous Mr. Hercules thought he could intimidate me - driving Mom's "MACH 3" (super-fast) GTO - NO WAY was I gonna back down from his nasty-azz 427 'Vette. I knew better: Of course, one would think..."Wow, a 425 horsepower 427 Corvette! What car could possibly even compete?"

Nope: In reality; with 425 horses "kicking" beneath the hood; a lightweight fiberglass Corvette would often - upon maximum acceleration - literally FISHTAIL and wheel-hop sideways to the curb.

Hence, in a street race, the winning car is NOT the one with the most horsepower; but rather the car delivering the MOST TORQUE to the rear wheels.

Herc - a really arrogant type - kept looking over at me condescendingly. To him I was another "sacrificial lamb"... about to be skewered by his behemoth Corvette.

But I figured he was in for an unpleasant surprise:

We were lined up at a red light: With a half-tank of Sunoco high-octane 260, I was thinking...

"Better put on your driving gloves Mr. Hercules: you're about to give that 4-speed shifter all it can handle."

Light goes green! Instantly Mom's GTO blasts out to an amazing one car lead! In my side mirror, I saw Herc with an "Oh sh*t I'm behind" facial expression.

I'd seen it a hundred times before. It was really funny-watching him"sweat."

In desperation, Hercules was power shifting- for all he was worth.

But not enough. When the GTO's automatic trans upshifted into final drive, the struggling corvette REMAINED one car length behind Mom's goat! Victory! A monster 427 vette - ignominiously biting the dust! Poor-poor Hercules: I knew he'd be jerked-off - LOSING in front of his chickie-poo. How embarrassing! - smoked by a "pig" GTO! Stopped beside me at the next red light, Hercules went nuclear: "If I hadda TUNE UP, Idda blown that M******* F****** pig GTO right off the *%$#*!**#*#^** road!"

Tsk-tsk. Such coarse language! Herc deserved to get his mouth "washed-out with soap."

Feigning diplomacy, I replied: "Yeah, sure man... No way I could beat your 'Vette all tuned up... Maybe we'll race again sometime," etc.

Immediately Herc chilled-out. I even saw a wisp of a SMILE as he drove away.

I thought: "How pathetic"... giving that 'I needa tune up' crap. Standard loser excuse. TIME CHECK: 11:30 pm... getting late:

Time to head for the "UNIVERSITY CLUB" on Belmont: a jammin' bar; always "packed to the rafters."

The U-Club always booked the best bands in the area. This particular band tonight - from nearby Sharon Pennsylvania - turned out to be real showstoppers. They had a big "following."

Through a dense cloud of cigarette smoke, I spotted a "cutie pie" - a petite redhead - seated at the bar.

"Hi! Haven't seen you around! Are you from Sharon?"

Apparently, she liked me! We "hit it off" - and began an animated conversation.

The band had begun their last set - playing "GRAZIN' IN THE GRASS" by the Friends of Distinction. No, she did not want to dance; but she seemed rather beguiled by my stories about Ohio State: I was bragging away - talking about going to Pasadena to the Rose Bowl. Being fraternity rush chairman...studying pre-med..."wild" frat parties...(blah-blah-blah), etc.

1 AM, I popped the question..."Needa ride home?"

"I'll tell my friends you're driving me."

YES!

I kept thinking..."Wait'll she sees Mom's gorgeous GTO!"

But I was shocked... she didn't seem impressed at ALL by the GTO.

That was a FIRST.

THEN, it really got "awkward."

Driving her home, she seemed to develop "lockjaw." (i.e.) quietly, she just sat in the bucket seat - staring blankly at the road ahead.

I thought..." Had I said something stupid?"

Turns out, she was being "coy" (i.e.) playing "hard to get."

"A little music MAESTRO."

I put on my favorite 8-track tape..."Best of the Lovin' Spoonful."

YEAH... that did the trick!

When "Summer in the City" came on, she lit up like Times Square..."Oh my gawd! My all-time FAVORITE song!"

Taking off her shoes- she put her bare feet up on the bucket seat: saying... "You know what...I haven't heard that song in

THREE YEARS!" Turns out that "Summer in the City" was indeed, for each of us, our "all time favorite song!"

La-dee-dah!

Could it be that LOVE was in the air?

Arriving at her house - PROBLEM - her 15-year-old brother was watching TV in the living room.

NOW WHAT?

Playing kissy-face on her living room couch was completely out of the question:

CURSES! My abominable luck with the ladies!

Would I now have to settle for a "passionate 'hand shake" on her front porch?

After a brief embrace - nothing left to do but head on home.

Exit stage right:

Then, at the last red light before the Ohio border... here

comes a black 68 442 convertible, 4-speed - two "farmers" aboard: They were laughing merrily - looking over at me like I was some hapless moron.

A 1968 442 Convertible

These two looked "Amish"- but they wore no hats. Probably had a copy of "The Farmer's Almanac" in the the glove box; with a pair of "trendy" Oshkosh overalls folded in the trunk: (love those suspenders). Both kept "smirking" at me - giddy with delight!

"Click-click... click-click... click-click." I could plainly hear the driver downshifting to 1st. Obviously, he couldn't wait to blow away another "hog-on-the-hoof" GTO!

They were really chortling away! But not for long:

It was high time to give these farmer gents an unobstructed look at the tail lights on Mom's GTO.

The light turned green: VAR-OOO-OOM! At 70 mph- looking in my mirror, I could barely see their headlights... at least 6 cars behind- maybe more! (ha-ha)

Now I imagined all the "creative" excuses this embarrassed 442 driver might be offering to his passenger:

"DAG-NABB that #*#$#!**% whipper-snapper in that #***##* GTO! If I hadda a tune-up, idda blown him right off the *%#@*#*!*% ROAD!"

QUOTE;

"Thou shalt not take the name of the Lord thy God in vain."

Chapter 26

AUGUST- 1969:

- One Thursday night, Mom called me to the phone - saying..."I think it's one of your fraternity brothers."

- It was the "Snake" - Allen Sellers - my wild 'n KRAZY fraternity brother- calling to

- remind me about his annual summer POOL party; this coming Saturday night.

- SNAKE: "You should've seen it last year, Ricky! There were way more chicks than guys!"

- ME: "Yeah, Snake...Saturday, around 9 pm. I'll see ya then."

Snake had grown up as the proverbial spoiled rich kid. His dad owned a thriving appliance store in downtown Beaver Falls, PA. One thing about Snake...he was unpredictable. Coming from money, he was "well-traveled."

At school - when Snake moved down the hall from me - immediately, he touched off STEREO WARS! He had an awesome Marantz 100 watt amp: JBL 12 inch speakers; Dual turntable: The best money could buy. But I had my family's trusty old record player; on which I always would play..."I am the Walrus."(koo-koo-ka-joo.)

From the third "animal" floor, one could hear Snake's BOOMING stereo halfway up the street! Snake - a lover of soul music - would always "serenade" the local area with the iconic, delightful... "I'm Black and I'm Proud" (James Brown) on

FULL VOLUME! Snake loved fireworks - keeping a wrinkled, brown bag of cherry bombs in his room. Seems that Snake had developed his own personal "JIHAD" vs. the hated Delts,

who's fraternity house was next door.

Occasionally, after returning from 2 AM "Last Call" - a highly-inebriated Snake would go up on the 4th floor roof - tossing a LIGHTED cherry bomb over onto the adjacent roof of the vile Delta house!

KAH-BOOOOOM! These were the loudest cherry bombs imaginable! They could have been used as military ordinance by the US Army in S. Vietnam: (e.g.) the sneaky Viet Cong - fleeing their underground tunnels - having suffered permanent hearing loss. (surrender or else)

Time check: Saturday 8 pm: I departed Youngstown - about 35 mInutes from Beaver Falls, PA. I had the top down... the 8 track blasting away. Directions in hand. La dee dah! A pool party!

Driving along, I had "visions of sugarplums" dancing in my head! It was those delightful words from Snake that kept ringing in my mind: "You should've seen it last year, Ricky."

There were way more CHICKS than guys!"

Ergo, I imagined a WILD, undisciplined affair...mobbed with bikini-clad hot ladies! - juiced on margaritas...cavorting around poolside! Driving through lovely, "pastoral" Pennsylvania - eager to get there- I decided to take a "short cut."

Not real smart:

Having the sense of direction of a blind man, I became lost on some dark, winding, densely-forested, 2 lane country road; with steep drops; and twisting, contorted upgrades. Help!...BOTH hands on the wheel!

Seeing all these spooky, yellow, deer-crossing signs, I feared a sudden collision with some horny, 13-point buck at any moment! I was actually scared. Where in the HELL was I? I'd never been so lost in my entire life. I'd become Ichabod Crane, riding through Spooky Hollow on Halloween eve.

AT LAST, I saw a sign with an arrow pointing..."Beaver Falls - 12 miles My "short cut" had resulted in my getting there in almost 1 1/2 hours, rather than 35 minutes.

Then, on the outskirts of Beaver Falls - disaster: It began to pour down rain. In fact, it began raining harder- then even harder! (cats 'n dogs) Scratch one pool party: (break out the awning).

I found Snake's house: Pulling into the long, curving driveway, I saw a few cars parked randomly; but not much else.

Walking up on the porch, Snake greeted me enthusiastically - saying, "Don't worry Ricky. I just called a bunch of people; they should be here pretty soon."

Man! What a RAUCOUS party! Somebody call the RIOT squad!

2 skinny guys - sitting "lotus position" in a corner - passing a "doobie" back 'n forth. In the kitchen, two stout, clean-cut males - fearlessly guarding the beer keg. Looking throughout the house...no more than 10 or 15 people milling about.

Yeah...Snake's prediction of "way more chicks than guys" seemed to have come up a tad short. It was either stay...or depart for a local nightclub? But Beaver Falls (East Podunk) wasn't exactly Palm Springs.

Then, Snake re-appeared...bottle of champagne in his hand. He knew I was ready to leave. "See ya later Snake"..."I'm heading back to Youngstown"..."Mom wants me home before midnight!"

"Ha -ha- hah." Snake was laughing as he walked me outside to the driveway:

"So this is your amazing goat?"

'Nope...It's my Mother's GTO. It's never been beat. Come up to Youngstown... we'll have a big showdown vs your 427 'vette." See ya at school next month. Arrivederci."

Exit stage right: Just my luck. The party had been a total bust. Like Frank always said..."Expect everything...get nothing."

Heading home, the closer I got to Youngstown, the more the rain subsided: All right! A race or two might yet be possible before the clock ran out.

For me, a night without racing, was like an alcoholic not drinking: I needed my BUZZ.

At last...Market street! It was 12 am.

The pavement was dry. No rain at all in the Youngstown area. INSTANTLY - up goes my "radar"- scanning for my first "target" this late Saturday evening. Then - as if a genie had fulfilled my wish- a white 66 442 came up alongside me: THREE occupants aboard. Driver acting like he's some real hot shot — looking over at me like I was some retarded moron - driving a "pig" GTO. I could read his arrogant facial expression... "Hah, another hoggy goat...I'll blow him away...my car ain't never been beat," etc.

Waiting at the red light, these three jokers were knee-slapping with laughter! A"pig" GTO was daring to race them! What a slaughter it was to be!

Then they turned down their radio: When the light jumped green- VA-ROOOOM! Mom's GTO bolted away so lightning-fast, Mr. 442, gave up after hitting 3rd gear - slowing down to a near crawl.

Then, I could NOT believe my eyes: At the next light, this lunatic 442 driver - overcome with embarrassment - ACTUALLY forced his two buddies out his passenger door - yelling over to me...."Now we'll have a FAIR RACE."

Imagine: viewing in my mirror the two hapless passengers, standing abandoned on the sidewalk - hands in their pockets - like 2 lost sheep!

UNBELIEVABLE! This 442 maniac was like some bullying night club bouncer! - kicking his two friends out of the car to lessen the weight! A desperado! A lunatic!

After lining up at the next red light with the 442; you can guess what happened: Yup; I beat him even WORSE - about 4 car lengths! (hah hah)

He drove off, back to his two stranded buddies: probably lying to them..."Yeah, I completely blew AWAY that jerk in that 69 GTO." etc. Heading toward downtown, I was thinking..."What a 3-ring circus that was!" The 442 driver seemed mad enough to chew nails, after I wiped him BADLY the second time! Plus; 66 442s were some of the fastest cars of the 60's; but not fast enough vs. Mom's devastating GTO! 1 AM, I saw a drop-dead-gorgeous, tuxedo black 68 SS 396 Chevelle in my mirror. With its blacked-out grill, and white accent stripes- running down over the rocker panels- it looked like it had just come off the showroom floor - obviously never been driven in winter. This 68 SS was an absolute killer, looks wise. (I still remember it today).

The black beauty pulled alongside me at the next red light: 2 well-dressed occupants (mid-20s -clean-cut) aboard. At once, they began snickering away - laughing about yet another "pig GTO," about to lose badly to their fearsome, NOISY, solid lifter L-78 Chevelle: 375 wild horses under the hood.... a street-monster!

Idling next to me, this noisy SS was shaking & shivering - like a hospital patient with the chills... banging-clanging away. With its solid-lifter camshaft, the loudly-clattering 396 engine sounded like a laundry dryer loaded with machine bolts. it was actually frightening. i was quaking with nervousness! So intimidating!

The SS driver looked arrogant, self-assured. His passenger - riding shotgun - was trying to smother his laughter! I was going to be their big chuckle for this Saturday night...or so they thought.

A '68 SS Chevelle

During the long red light - It was pure suspense; this L-78 SS Chevelle - clattering LOUDLY with those solid lifters – was enough to TERRIFY anyone who pulled alongside at a red light. NOTE: From '66 on, Chevrolet had made the L-78 1965 Corvette engine (425 hp) optional on their SS Chevelle. Cleverly- to placate car insurance companies - they'd rated this exact same 425 hp engine @ 375 hp. The L-78 SS Chevelle was indeed "the big-bad-wolf" of 60's muscle cars. Bearing an ACTUAL 425 hp, they could BLOW AWAY almost anything! Many a street racer would cringe in fear - whenever lining up with an L-78. (me too)

Light changes to green! GAR-OO-O-O-O-O-OM!

Instantly, the sleek front end of the 4-speed Chevelle lifted violently upward – roaring like thunder. Wow! - it was incredibly LOUD! I looked over at the guy riding shotgun. He was laughing no longer - acting like he was riding in a wooden roller coaster - holding on for dear life! His eyes - wide open with astonishment.

It was, indeed, a high-intensity, pulse-pounding matchup between 2 super-fast MUSCLE cars! Once again, Mom's rocket GTO was quicker: the SS Chevelle - stubbornly "clinging" to my rear bumper - was unable to make up the 1 car shortfall. Now I was the one trying to smother my laughter! I'd given these 2 hotshots the surprise of their lives. Yeah, man! So sweet!

At the next light, the two cocky guys - looking totally dumbfounded – were rather gracious in defeat - looking over at me, shaking their heads in complete astonishment.

"Wow...that's a pretty good running goat! Is that ram air?"

"Nope. It's a stock 400/350. It's my Mother's GTO."

U- wanna race again?"

But just before we got the green light, some soporific moron - driving about 10 mph - pulled out in front of us from a lonely side street. Probably some wine head in a stupor behind the wheel. Too bad. No second race would take place. Woulda been amazing to wipe out a mighty L-78 Chevelle TWICE in one night...something "I could tell to my grandchildren." Indeed, if there existed a "Muscle Car Hall of Fame," Mom's rocket-fast goat would have been voted in UNANIMOUSLY on the first ballot!

On this night, Mom's GTO was indeed "king of the asphalt jungle."

"LONG LIVE THE KING."

Chapter 27

SEPTEMBER 1969:

By late summer '69, cultural and societal changes had come to the forefront: America's teenagers no longer wanted to act young: Hence, they'd decided to become "more involved." (i.e.) reject the so-called "Establishment" for a new societal order:

Therefore, spread messages about Love. Peace. Racial Harmony. Be more "introspective." Discover one's "inner self"...etc.

QUOTE:

"I don't have a job; but what I'm doing is important...promoting peace (Vietnam). Saving the world from destroying itself."

(i.e.) an often-heard pathetic excuse, for justifying one's addiction to SMOKING POT - usually at all hours.

QUOTE:

"I'm always stoned. But it's better than being an alcoholic."

Evidence of this new "school of thought" abounded: Fast food parking lots were deserted after dark. Red Barn was empty. People wearing bell-bottoms - growing beards. Longer hair with sideburns was "cool."

Hippie culture was "far out."

Police - much like GTOs - were now "pigs."

Stopped at red lights, the pungent odor of "wacky-tobbacky" could be detected from an adjacent car. One night, I'd heard that there was a party on the Northside. "Hey, why not? Maybe, a few lovely ladies might be in attendance."

Walking into the party, I spotted Walter Podolski; who'd played tennis with me on our high school team. We shook hands...so glad to see each other!

ME: "Hey Wally...where ya been all summer?"

WALLY: "I'm a fireman on the Erie Lackawanna." (A lucrative railroad job - requiring 7-day, 60 hour work weeks).

I felt "relieved" - Wally had NOT morphed into some slovenly, pot-addled jerk; unlike many of my old friends, who'd become aimless in their lives. Wally was happy: "I just bought a 68 Vette! I had it going 130 out by the airport! But I never drive it to work."

Unlike me, Wally wasn't a drag racer. So I said nothing about street-racing. But I DID tell Wally I was driving a new 69 GTO.

ME: "Let's go for a quick spin out Market. I just bought 'Best of Jimi Hendrix." This goat has a factory 8-track!"Walking out to the street, Wally seemed astonished - opening the passenger door:

"Wow Ricky. Is this car yours?"

"Nope: It's my Mother's GTO... It's a screamer! Maybe we'll race someone on Market. You'll be amazed."

Now, it was "nostalgia" time:

We remembered playing tennis as kids: Wally had "the fastest first serve." But he never bragged about anything. It was always fun to hang around with him.

Traveling down 5th Ave, we spotted Jerry "the Bug" Perelman - hitch hiking. His parents had been customers on my old paper route, back when I was 14. I had known Jerry since he was an impish 8 year old. Now in high school - he'd evolved into a "laid-back" hippie; with LONG "hippie" hair. Standing at curbside, Bug looked as if he'd just started military "boot" camp.

ME: "Bug! – what HAPPENED to your hair?"

BUG: "Was hitch-hiking home from Woodstock...some New York cops busted me with pot... they were pricks! They shaved my head and threw me in jail...had to call my parents to bail me out...God, how I hate cops; they're all PIGS!" etc.

Wally was trying not to laugh at the Bug's new "buzz-cut." With his big round nose, Bug resembled "Uncle Fester" from the "Addams Family."

BUG: "Where you guys headed?"

ME: "Out Market."

BUG: "COOL! Could you take me to the Green Dragon? They stay open till midnight."

"Hop in." It was dusk, around 8 pm.

"Green Dragon" was Youngstown's original "head" shop. Seems that Bug had run out of "zig-zags" - this was before rolling papers were sold everywhere.

We certainly made a strange threesome driving out Market street. Bug was in back, rummaging through my eight track tapes, scattered on the seat.

BUG: "Cool! "Crosby, Stills and Nash"- play this one. You've got some really far out tapes man." No matter what was said to him, Bug's response was "far out" or 'cool'... a rather restricted vocabulary. Bug asked Wally..."Got any spare change?"

As we drove up to the "head shop," a hanging sign was on the front door: "SH*T. They're closed." I had to laugh about Bug. He had that "maddening self assurance." No matter the situation, Bug would "take charge."

Minutes later - crossing into Boardman township - Bug asked me to plug in the cigarette lighter.

"What for?"

He fumbled through his pockets - holding what looked like a small brown pebble:

BUG: "This is blonde hash.... cost 20 bucks."

When the lighter popped out, Bug plunked his hash onto the red-hot lighter coils - "snorting" away - inhaling deeply - holding his breath.

"A-h-h...want some?"Bug made a forward gesture with the smoldering lighter. We both declined. He was making me and Wally nervous. After his next big snort, Bug seemed content..."A-h-h... this stuff is the best."

Then, without warning, brilliant red strobe lights began flashing about 30 yards behind us! It was a dreaded OHIO HIGHWAY patrol car!

"COPS! Oh sh*t" Bug immediately chucks his hash out the window - a look of terror on his face! Pulling over, I was in panic mode! I pictured court rooms. Lawyers. A criminal record! Accused of a felony drug violation!

I knew the lingering hash smell would cause the cop to call for a "drug-sniffing" dog. Looking in my mirror, I see the cop - wearing his traditional "Smokey" bear hat - sauntering up to my window. God, what trouble would I be in! I pictured being "strip-searched."

COP: "Good evening Sir...may I see your driver's license?"

"What for, officer?"

"Your license plate bulb is burned out...I'll have to write you a warning. No penalty or fine. But you need to get that replaced."

Minutes later, after cop wrote his "warning," he drove off:

"WHEW"- I felt this HUGE sense of relief.

Damm! I could've practically STRANGLED the Bug; with his indolent, hippie lifestyle. NEVER AGAIN would I have anything to do with him.

Poor Wally: He'd nearly "soiled" his pants - trying to recover his breath. His face had turned pale.

What if he'd lost his railroad job? It had indeed been a really close call - courtesy of some anal, nit-picky, Ohio state trooper.

And the Bug? He was angrily bemoaning the loss of his blonde hash "investment"...laying 50 yards back near a sewer at curbside.

BUG: " Twenty bucks...DOWN the #*#!*## drain... I hate #*%##** cops! They're ALL a buncha PIGS."

WALLY: "We coulda been in a lot of trouble, man."

ME: "Hey Bug...still living at home?"

WALLY: "Maybe the party's still going."

I headed back to the North side...it had been a really "far out" time.

Chapter 28

May 7, 1970:

After the horrific Kent State shootings, Ohio Governor James Rhodes declared all state universities would close indefinitely, until everything 'COOLED OFF."

FINALLY! A much-desired break from Ohio State; and all those dreaded, obnoxious, student "PEACE" protesters. Throwing rocks, shouting obscenities - breaking windows; they were about as peaceful as Attila the Hun. Some were heaving bricks! The "F-word" always on their lips.

Most were outside agitators - the dreaded "SDS" (Students for a Democratic Society). Nevertheless; It was HIGH time to get outta Columbus ASAP! Parts of campus seemed like an undeclared "WAR ZONE."

Not much later, Snake and I - in his 69 gold 427 'vette - were heading home to Youngstown OH; and Beaver Falls PA - arguing all the way about who's car was FASTER.

SNAKE: "My Vette ain't never been beat, Ricky."

"NEVER?" said I.

"NEVER" said the Snake.

"You'll see."

We pulled into my driveway - making it official: We'd have the "race to end all races"...his 427 Corvette vs. Mom's GTO. I gave Snake "fair warning"...his mighty-mighty 427 Vette could be in for a surprise butt-whippin! I had it ALL planned: I was gonna serve the Snake a generous piece of humble pie! I went see the

O'Neal brothers...genuine "grease under the nails" car technicians; who'd give Mom's GTO special treatment (i.e.) an advanced, state-or-the-art SUPER tune-up.

A '69 Corvette Convertable

Both Joe and Mike O'Neal were my high school friends. I always talked cars with them during lunch. They loved Chevies: they were the "go to guys" for working on any Chevrolet.

Nevertheless- being highly capable - they could super-tune ANY GM engine, including a 400 cubic inch Pontiac GTO. The O'Neals really DID KNOW "every trick in the book."

That night, I drove over to their expanded, backyard garage. When they saw Mom's goat, they flipped-out..."Wow Ricky, when did you get THAT?

"It's my Mother's GTO. I need you guys to make it run perfect. Hasn't been tuned since last summer."

After giving them money for the necessary parts; they'd installed hotter spark plugs.Hi-capacity ignition wires. New dual-point distributor with advanced timing: also, they expertly blocked off the heat riser valve.

Lastly, they "re-calibrated" the 4- barrel Quadra-jet carburetor - like two surgeons in an operating chamber. It was riveting watching them - acting with total precision.

Using special mini-Phillips screw drivers - turning the tiny adjustment screws ever so gently - they listened intently to the "whooshing" sound coming through the jets of the big-diameter Rochester 4 barrel carb. Suddenly, they BOTH nodded approval - saying..."Ricky; just watch how it runs NOW." I thought..."these guys are amazing...mechanical superstars!"

Actual WIZARDS in my estimation. Next, the road test. I punched the gas and WOW: the GTO's front end violently jerked upward! The rear tires broke loose - laying a huge 10 foot strip! I could smell the acrid tire smoke. Truly an amazing improvement! I was jubilant!

Mom's GTO ran FASTER than new! I didn't think it'd be possible. It seemed "transformed."

Ha-ha! Snake would NOW be in for the surprise of his life!

Snake called: it was all set: 12:30 AM that next Friday night. We'd meet halfway at the Shell station, adjacent to the Route 11 Columbiana County entrance ramp; equidistant between Youngstown and Beaver Falls (PA).

Time Check: Friday night-12:30 AM. Both Snake and I were psyched for the big show-down...waiting for all the freeway traffic to subside.

Mom's GTO was running on hi-octane Sunoco 260 - not too different from AVIATION GASOLINE! (plus a super tune)

It was almost 1 AM. Traffic gone. Rt. 11 was now clear.

"Gentlemen...Start your engines." Snake was in the left lane - overconfident- laughing OBNOXIOUSLY; not at all aware of the surprise that awaited him: I played the starter - without his green flag.

"Okay Snake...we'll go on THREE!"

"One...two...THREE"

WHOOOOOOOOM...The front end of Snake's monster corvette violently jerked upward. But incredibly, I bolted away to a ONE CAR lead!

The side-pipes from the Corvette's 427 engine were literally emitting green-yellow plumes of flame! So unbelievably LOUD! (forgot my earplugs)

Now, Snake was no longer laughing. Glancing in my left mirror, Snake's facial expression was..."Oh sh*t! I'm behind!"

At 70 mph I was still one car ahead. Then, at 80, I saw him closing FAST.

"Oh sh*t! Here he comes."

Finally, he caught me around 100 mph. Immediately, I took my foot off the gas, as Snake's gold Corvette began pulling away. Ahead, Snake had pulled off to the roadside - looking totally bewildered: obviously, the first time he'd ever raced a super-fast car, like Mom's GTO.

I pulled up to Snake; he seemed a sore loser:

SNAKE: "Why'd you back off Ricky? You took your foot off the gas!"

ME: "Snake. I beat you up to 100; that's approximately a quarter mile...c'mon... admit it."

But Snake would admit NOTHING. Delusionally thinking he was the winner, because he had passed me at 100 mph. Suddenly...brilliant blue-red revolving lights! - 30 yards up-road. Another dreaded Ohio Highway Patrol officer! He came walking up towards us, flashlight in hand.

COP: "Good evening...Is there some problem here?"

ME: "No problem officer; just getting directions."

This cop was "dedicated." Most certainly he'd broadcast an all-points: "Be on the LOOKOUT for a green 69 GTO and gold 69 corvette - engaging in an illegal highway race."

It was time to "get out of Dodge"...no second race would take place. We both drove off. Nevertheless, it was the ONE time in my life when I was GLAD to see an OHIO State trooper.

I wanted no part of any second race with Snake's behemoth 427 corvette. It was a monster!

I had to laugh... "saved" by some Ohio State patrol cop. I had antipathy toward them ALL. They'd give a ticket to their own mother if she exceeded a "safe speed" on a highway.

FLASHBACK: I recalled 3 years ago: June, '67. I had received a personal letter at home.

Dad wanted to know..."Who's Sue Summerdale?"

It was the name on the return address...from Akron OH.

Curious, I began reading it.

Turns out that Sue Summerdale had been my 'BLIND DATE" from a fraternity party, back in late May in 1967 - something I'd forgotten completely. I NOW recalled the "night of THAT party"- being NEAR-TERRIFIED...waiting in the women's dormitory lobby - expecting the absolute WORST.

Most of my blind dates had been COMPLETE disasters: Some would have a "voice like a man." Others would have thick, stumpy legs: upon FIRST seeing them, my initial inclination was to bolt for the door, and RUN AWAY! With so many ill-fated encounters with "fix-up dates," I was PRAYING this next "blind" date wouldn't resemble the "Bride of Frankenstein." (get ready to run)

But when Sue got off the dormitory elevator, she was kinda "cute" with EXCELLENT legs! My best blind date ever! (She seemed very pleased with me)

Arriving at the party, we sat with my "big brother." All new pledges were assigned a big brother.

It was Mike Atwood, from Kettering OH. He had a quart bottle of Thunderbird, ice cold.

Trick was, if a pack of grape Kool aid was mixed in, it would kill the glycol (antifreeze) taste (i.e.) it became "palatable."

We shared turns- "chugging" its contents in less than two minutes. It went down like grape FANTA.

Initially, it had a "laxative" effect. I remember looking in the mirror of the men's room- looking as if I was wearing purple lip stick - stained from the grape Kool Aid.

The band played "KNOCK ON WOOD" (Eddie Floyd). MY all time favorite dance song.

Soon, I was no longer dancing like a "white guy." The buzz was kicking in. I had discovered my "natural rhythm."

After that, I was "wiped out." Next day, Mark Hyland told me that he'd carried me "unconscious" into my room - having no memory of the night before. I was shocked reading Susie's letter: She was writing to THANK me for the great time at the party; and was extending an "invitation" to visit next Saturday at her home...her parents away for that weekend. For one thing, I didn't even remember taking Susie to her dorm afterwards. Obviously, she got my home address from the Ohio State Directory of Students. In the letter she mentioned my "great sense of humor"... and that "I reminded her SO much of her older brother" who also was humorous.

She wrote that "she had fun all that night" - laughing at my purple lips...adding, "it was the best party I'd ever been to."

Damm. What a fool was I: If I hadn't gotten so foolishly drunk that night, I could've - like a gentleman - brought her back to her dorm, STILL STANDING upright.

Next Saturday, I drove to Akron in our 62 Bonneville. It was 8 pm.

Susie had dinner waiting: We spent a nice "chummy" evening at her home. It was 2 am. I had a one hour drive back to Youngstown- most of it traveling on the newly-opened I-76 freeway.

Fighting drowsiness, I was going about 80. The night was "murky." Visibility poor. No other vehicles on the road.

Then, in my mirror, way-way back I saw headlights...obviously a sneaky Ohio Highway patrol man. (who else)

I slowed down to 50. The taillights on the Bonneville looked dim in the thick fog.

Suddenly, this over-eager cop comes nearly crashing into me from behind! – not aware of my slowing down. He stayed RIGHT behind me (10 feet). CAREFUL. We drove for about 3 miles: The cop was loving the opportunity to "wield" his authority.... hugging my bumper.... headlights bright in my mirror; while probably running license plate checks - looking intently for safety violations. ANY pretext to pull me over.

Then strangely, this cop puts on his "right turn" signal - driving off at the Kent-Ravenna exit. It was obvious to me...why would he signal a right turn? No one behind. I was ahead of him. No other traffic around.

I could read his mind: I traveled ahead about a 1/4 mile; extinguished my lights - pulling off to the side: Looking intently in my mirror at the entrance ramp...waiting for only a minute.

Sure enough I saw headlights: Guess who? This sneaky cop comes FULL SPEED down the entrance ramp- "RRRRRRRRR"- zooming by me parked off to the side - looking determined!

I pulled back onto I-76.

Now, I was BEHIND him.

Nice try Sherlock.

This cop's crafty attempt to ambush me for speeding went for naught: I'd completely outwitted this perverse, sadistic "officer of the law" - who probably was the schoolyard 6th-grade bully; then went on to greater glory as a gung-ho bunghole, highway patrol cop.

Plus, I'd saved myself the disaster of 75 dollar speeding ticket- equal to 700 dollars in today's currency... essentially for doing nothing WRONG! God, how I despised Ohio Highway Patrolmen. They were the worst thing about living in Ohio. I now realized that Ohio Highway Patrolmen were nothing other than REVENUERS - going to any extreme to write speeding tickets. Totally deplorable! Perhaps I might one day run for Governor: My first day in office? Save the taxpayers a real "boatload" of money...I would disband the entire Ohio Highway Patrol.

"TEN FOUR"

Chapter 29

SPRING - 1970:

By now, muscle car MANIA was like an all-consuming fire. It was out of control!

The messages were EVERYWHERE:

Turn on your TV and there she'd be! "Mean Mary Jean" (in her foxy micro-skirt) - crowing away about Dodge's new "Scat Pack" cars - ALL with Chrysler's molten-hot 340 V8. They were lightning-fast! - zero to 60.

Nevertheless, by this time, it had become a wild, daring game of..."Can You Top This?"- much like an automotive "arms race." Every auto manufacturer was cranking out some faster-hotter-newer model - designed SPECIFICALLY for BLOWING AWAY the competition at red lights.

In car magazines, I'd read about the "GSX" - Buick's blistering-fast new muscle car - clocking the amazingly quick time of 13.19 (seconds) in the quarter mile! Not too shabby. Ever since I was a bratty little kid, I HATED Buicks. Even that name "Buick" sounded weird to me.

Back in the 1950s, my Aunt Nellie - a school teacher - drove a black 1952 Buick Roadmaster. This car had a funny smell; and was butt-ugly. I HATED riding in it. To me, a Buick "muscle car" was an oxymoron! FLASHBACK 1965: I remembered our neighbor, Mr. Levy, with his new, white, 1965 Buick GRAN SPORT parked in his driveway. His punk, 19 year old son (Mitchell) would drive it around the neighborhood, like he was some sort of "hell-on-wheels."

It was laughable! I'd watch Mitchy driving by - his left elbow out the window - acting like he's some total bad-azz - trying to "show-off."

Evidently, Mitchell thought wheeling around town in daddy's new Gran Sport, would "transform" him - from the ultimate cretin - into Mr. COOL.

Even when we were kids - hanging out at the park on our Schwinn bicycles - nurdy Mitchell would come along - showing off his "English-racer" bike; with all those wires on the handle bars. (i.e.) those were the brakes.

As the old saying goes..."Child is father to the man."

Word was, that Mitchell - with his great-big "Groucho Marx" nose - had the "hots" for Loretta Berman. A real scream among the neighborhood cronies! Since his father owned a delicatessen on Belmont, Mitchy considered himself "eligible." Hence, Mitch had decided he'd compete for "the hand" of lovely Loretta. His "plan" was to drive daddy's new Gran Sport past her house; and

THAT would get him noticed. Poor-poor Mitchy (tsk tsk). Endlessly, he would drive past Loretta's house...at all times; at all hours: all to no avail.

It was Saturday 6 PM: I was going to the Belmont Sunoco gas station; then I'd head on out to Market street.

Mom's bad-to-the-bone GTO was still untied & unbeaten after a year - incredible! But the sand was running through the hourglass: How much longer could this amazing streak last?

Then, on impulse, I decided to give a ring to my "almost" girlfriend in Sharon PA. The one I'd met last summer - a real cutie pie (with alluring red hair).

Over the school year, I'd written her a few "almost" love letters; so it wouldn't be a total surprise.

She answered the phone: at home doing nothing. It was all set: I'd pick her up at 8, then we'd check out a movie.

"Maybe I can talk her into a DRIVE-IN"...Yes!

Arriving on time, she was waiting on the porch.

But she wanted to see the 2nd run of "Cactus Flower," with Goldie Hawn and Walter Matthau.

I decided to wimp out (i.e.) not argue with her. Now, the drive-in was OUT. Already, it was apparent: I was becoming a compliant, pussy-whipped moron! (play Four Tops "I Can't Help Myself") The theater was 15 minutes away.

So we sang along with the 8-track, and to my delight, she had a sarcastic sense of humor! I was beguiled.

A chick that could make ME laugh? La-dee-dah... Could LOVE be in the air? Turning onto some busy thoroughfare, we were stopped at the first red light. Then I heard..."click-click...click-click...click-click" — the unmistakable sound of a 4-speed transmission - being downshifted into first (gear).

In the right lane was a "beat-up" white 65 442 - driven by this sleazy-looking guy (early 30s) with a taciturn facial expression.

He was hard to "read." His 442 looked like a "work car." The driver - staring blankly ahead- seemed "unconcerned"...and NO radio playing.

Puzzled, I decided to ignore this car altogether. Bad hunch: The light had turned yellow for the intersecting street: Then, this sneaky 442 driver caught me "sleeping at the switch."

Cleverly, he punched the gas a split second BEFORE the green light....already a half car length in front.

Outraged, immediately I stomped on the gas, and the GTO bolted ahead past him.

"GR-ROOOOOOOOM." It was almost a dead-even race! He kept even with my passenger door - a real nail biter!

And this was no ordinary driver! He power-shifted through his gears like a professional NHRA drag racer...KA-HING...KA-HING...KA-HING. This guy was determined to win!

It was a quarter mile to the next red light. The 442 could not pull even. It turned out to be one of the most dramatic, rousing, street races I'd had in a long time: a real heart-pounder! The 442 made a right turn - disappearing down a side street.

I looked over at Cutie Pie, who seemed a bit perturbed. I was taken aback by her reaction:

"Do you HAVE to do that?"

"Do what?"

"Drag racing like some high school nut. How immature! Grow up."

After that, she clammed up tight- not saying another word. She seemed to be really upset. I was shocked! Bewildered...WTF?

Just because of some inconsequential, spur-of-the-moment, 20-second street race, she'd transformed from Cutie pie into an impertinent little snip.

Obviously, no longer was "love in the air." I felt like I was "walking on eggs"...having no idea at all what to say to her...totally befuddled.

Throughout the insipid movie - which I despised - she hardly gave me a glance (i.e.) the silent treatment.

Damm...Dwight Patterson had it right all along..."Ya gotta treat 'em like shet."

On the way home, she seemed to "thaw out" a little. As I approached her street, we were on "speaking terms."

But still, I felt resentment. Why be a nasty b*tch over some insignificant, meaningless street race?

Courage: I decided to man up...enough is enough. "Nicey-nice" just didn't work. No more being pussy-whipped.

Time to "retaliate."

At her front door, her body language said... "do come in."

Sorry dear:

I gave her a perfunctory..."I'll be calling you... g'night." I then jumped "triumphantly" into the GTO - burning RUBBER all the way down her street!

YEAH. I felt a sense of relief. Time to hit Market Street and satisfy my need for speed!

It was 11:35 pm. On Saturday nights, Market St. would be rocking 'n rolling! With all its steel jobs, Youngstown was boomtown, USA!

After a 35 minute trip, I arrived at Market st. - just after midnight. PERFECT TIMING: people & cars everywhere - acting like "the war is over!"

The bars had long lines outside. An aura of festivity. Youngstown's own little Mardi Gras.

I'm sure little Miss Cutie Pie was wondering if she had chosen the "right card to play" - expecting me to meekly apologize at her door to get a little "lovey-dovey."

Then it dawned upon me...she was an ACTRESS! A real pro at keeping any potential new boyfriend on the defensive. After all, I wasn't drag racing on "Dead Man's Curve," so why her big outrage? And I fell for it!

Cruising up Market, I spotted a garish, canary-yellow 1970 Olds Cutlass at a red light with huge trumpet dual exhausts and oversized tires.

A '70 Cutlass Rally 350

"Hmmm. What's this?" Something new?

This flashy Oldsmobile looked like it could really haul azz. Lined up aside the Cutlass, I saw its distinctive logo..."Rally 350." Rally 350? Hardy har! This "RALLY 350" driver, about 19, was an arrogant, egotistical punk - looking over at me disdainfully - like he was king of the road.

Time to de-throne the king! Light changed to green! The Rally 350 came out fast; just behind me; but around 50 mph, the GTO effortlessly pulled away! (ha-ha) Another one bites the dust! (play QUEEN song)

Next, was a dreaded 1969 340 Dart Swinger (orange) at Market & Auburndale; an ideal intersection for a race.

Looking over, the driver - about 25 - was reminiscent of Harrison Ford in "American Graffiti." Mr. Arrogance himself.

A '69 Dodge Dart Swinger 340

He gave a nasty, contemptuous glance over at me - with a cocksure facial expression...defiant posture...haughty attitude. I pointed forward with my right index finger - indicating...wanna race?

Disdainfully, he retorts..."Unless you wanna go for five, I wouldn't waste my time."

What a consummate jerk! - giving me that "unless we race for money" crap. A totally conceited bunghole! He drove away.

Approaching 2 AM; traffic became sparse. I was a bit frustrated. Despite all the driving around, there was no one left to race. Time expired... forced to go home.

While heading home, I began to think better about Cutie pie: Finally, I had her figured out: She was a control freak. After all, what better to control someone, than keep 'em guessing & wondering (i.e.) off-balance. Which is EXACTLY what I had done all that night- guessing & wondering what was going through her mind. Kind of clever when you think about it: It's just like winning at poker. Never ever show your CARDS (i.e.) never let the other one know what you're thinking. Indeed, Cutie pie could have been nominated for an Oscar - for her "stirring performance." Damm. I wondered - if not for her seductive red hair - I just might've said "bon voyage" and gone about my merry (lunatic) way - as "the Mad Dragster of Market Street".

God, what a conundrum: Going with Cutie pie meant NO MORE racing from red lights (i.e.) being pussy-whipped all over again. Is that any way to live?

QUOTE:

"NO MAN CAN SERVE TWO MASTERS"

Chapter 30

May 1970 - Week 3:

The Kent State riots now over, Ohio Governor Jim Rhodes called all state universities back in session. OSU students now returned to their classes.

Snake - after racing Mom's GTO - seemed to be ignoring my calls about a ride back to OSU: (sore loser) Lucky for me, Pauly Sackerman, also a senior at Ohio State - was available as my "backup" driver.

Pauly - living next door - was my childhood buddy.

Being an "impressionable" 7 year-old kid, Pauly's 3rd floor attic seemed like PARADISE! So many FUN things to do! Pauly's Lionel electric train was my favorite. Then we'd play Clue. Sorry. Chinese checkers. Bumper pool. Chutes & Ladders. Chess. Checkers. Electric football. All Star Baseball. Monopoly...all the coolest games from that time.

Every Saturday during winter, I would be over to play: We'd play all day on Saturday, except for lunch.

Pauly's Mom NEVER would offer me something to eat; plus, their kitchen was unkempt. Even worse, they'd allow their pathetically stupid dog to slurp water from the toilet: YECK. I kept waiting for it to get sick or drop dead, but somehow, it survived.

Playing Monopoly, I had to watch Pauly. He took a "stealth" approach to playing. Every time he passed GO, he'd try to collect 300 dollars, which is why he'd ALWAYS insist on being the banker. Often, when distracted - reading a "Chance" or "Community

Chest" card - he'd try to slide a 500 from the bank's money to under HIS side of the board (i.e.) "now you see it; now you don't." Pauly loved to play stupid, pukey, boring "Scrabble." Not only did I hate that INSIPID game, I despised its stupid NAME!

Scrabble? What a stupid, weirdo name! Who's idea was that? It sounded like an insecticide: "Gotta problem with ants? Get SCRABBLE."

As time went by, Pauly - once an okay friend - had weirdly devolved into this bizarre world of his own making (i.e.) He took a perverse delight from torturing insects.

With a demonic look on his face, Pauly LOVED pulling wings off flies - giving him a sense of "mastery" over another living thing.

Mysteriously, he would become spellbound watching spiders. He seemed capable of "communicating" with them (i.e.) The "Spider Whisperer."

He'd be watching them intently for hours - weaving their sticky webs all over his cellar window screens.

Not surprisingly, kids in the neighborhood would never go near him. But Pauly - with his huge pile of D.C. and Marvel comic books - in summertime, would stay in his garage all day, reading happily away to his heart's content. The fact that he collected baseball cards validated that he was somewhat "normal."

Anyway, Pauly was really glad to have a passenger aboard for the not-so-exciting, 3 hour ride back to "fun city" Columbus, "Ohia." (hillbilly heaven). Riding down Interstate 71, I was preoccupied, thinking about Cutie pie..." torn between 2 loves."

She hated drag racing. Ergo, getting serious with this little miss would require me to forego all RACING from red lights. No way would I ever agree to THAT. I decided to play "hard to get." No calling little Cutie pie for ANY reason whatsoever.

After spring quarter, arriving home for summer, I was greeted with a rather shocking surprise: Instead of Mom's GTO, I saw a crappy, chintzy, crummy Opel Kadette in the garage. (i.e.) A little pipsqueak foreign auto exported from West Germany.

Mom said it was a "rental,"- explaining that my show-off sister had wrecked the GTO - speeding around Mill Creek Park with a carload of friends. Luckily, the GTO wasn't "totaled."

The Opel's chintzy interior felt like plastic. The gas gauge was in liters. This car looked cheap, to the point of embarrassment. Upon starting it up, the Opel's engine sounded much like my grandma's sewing machine - "whirring" away.

Not exactly a fearsome, tire-scorching muscle car. It looked (and sounded) wimpy...a "muscle" Opel Kadette!

No WAY did I want anyone to see me driving it around ANYWHERE.

At the Pontiac body shop, the GTO had the frame intact; but the front was almost gone...a "survivor car."

"When do you think it' 'll be ready?"

"Not for at least 3 more weeks," replied the body shop manager. Walking up to Frank's house was another shock: In his driveway was a crappy, crummy Volkswagen BUG rather than his sleek 66 Corvette.

The much-abused 'Vette needed a new engine AND clutch. Said Frank..."I didn't have the money to get it fixed. Some used car guy offered me an even trade for a VW." And what an awesome VW: Could barely do 30 up a hill! A total PIECE OF SHEET! Disgusting!

Hence, NO more cruising Market Street, at least until July.

So at night, we'd sit in Frank's VW - parked at McDonald's on Belmont - sipping Ripple wine - singing merrily along with the AM radio top-40 hits.

After July 4th, Mom's goat was ready. The GTO looking showroom new!

That next Friday night, I could not wait to hit Market Street. But Mom and Dad were taking Aunt Mary to dinner...it was her 60th birthday.

Next day (Saturday) Mom's goat got the "showroom" treatment. I even cleaned out the trunk, underneath the seats, under the hood: everywhere.

Saturday night, Market Street was action central! Hot cars zooming around. Horns honking. Traffic heavy. Frank and I were "cleared for action."

Always looking intently in my rearview mirror (street racer's survival rule #1), I was aware of this lurid yellow car- mixed in with the dense column of traffic- trailing me at a distance.

Suddenly, I realized an aggressive Buick GSX driver had been STALKING me all the way out Market Street!

A 1970 Buick GSX

BATTLE STATIONS!

He quickly maneuvered up beside me- acting like a World War 2 fighter ace- hell bent on "shooting me down."

Then it HIT me! This GSX jockey was ME- exactly one summer ago! It was like deja vu turned "outside-in."

Driving out of Market back in '69, I had become maniacal - hunting down Roadrunners, SS Chevelles, and 440 RT Chargers. GTXs. Superbees, 396 Camaros, 442s, Corvettes - everything.

I would see one and "go after 'em" like a bloodhound after an escapee - completely mesmerized by the sheer SPEED of Mom's GTO, which, inevitably, led to my blowing them ALL away!

If you lined up vs. a "PIG" GTO, you EXPECTED to easily blow its doors off.

But by summer 69, with the proliferation of the sizzling-hot GTO Judge - with its fierce Ram Air III engine - it was most certainly NOT a pig.

Pontiac 400 Ram Air engines were designed for all hard-core street racers- not to be MESSED with unless you were primed for a nasty street encounter.

And now, this Buick hot-shot was on his own personal power trip, just like me a year before. Behind the wheel of a GSX meant nothing to fear.

The GSX's 455 cubic inch monster engine was massive - having the MOST torque of any car available on the market.

And GSX Buicks lived up to their hype...faster than "all-get-out" in the quarter mile. Looking over at this hotshot GSX driver beside me; he was acting cocky. Arrogant. Self-assured. His passenger riding shotgun, likewise. This "stylishly dressed" driver (about 21-22) acted totally complacent. Probably some spoiled rich kid whose Daddy bought him his dream car...a new GSX. Looking over at these two characters, they actually seemed BORED (i.e.)"Ho-hum...another day at the office...blow the doors off another pig GTO; then head to the water cooler."

As much as I HATED Buicks, this yellow GSX was absolutely stunning. The best looking and fastest Buick ever!

The traffic thinned out. We were lined-up at an IDEAL red light: a quarter mile until the next signal - slightly uphill.

Frank - having no idea about any GSX - wasn't anticipating a close race at all.

But the SUSPENSE was apparent. It was a long red light. During the interim, Frank had been bantering with the GSX driver:

"HE WANTS TO RACE FOR 5 BUCKS."

"WHAT?"

"Just RACE him....I'll put up the five bucks." Frank pulled out a five and waved it at the driver, who nodded "yes."

Not again! Never could I understand that "race for 5 bucks" crap.

Five bucks? Wow! Big deal! Was 5 bucks REAL MONEY for anyone? What difference could 5 dollars make to any muscle car driver? Was it to be a part of his "secure retirement" income? Utterly ridiculous! (save your money for a rainy day) Suddenly, the light changed to green! "G-R-R-R-R-O-O--O-W"...the GSX came screaming out of the chute...front end lifted high! My God! Was it ever fast! Mom's GTO kept dead even: bumper-to-bumper - all the way up to 100 MPH... incredible! This GSX - running with its front end angled high over the street - was testimony to the prodigious torque of its "Stage One" monster engine. Evidently, the GSX driver seemed shocked. Pulling alongside, he was shaking his head - asking..."That's not a ram air, is it?"

"Nope...this is my Mother's GTO."

"Let's race again."

It was like "instant replay." Upon green, Mom's GTO jumped out to a 10-foot lead. The GSX's headlights were at my right front door; but he just could NOT pull even.

Frank - riding shotgun - was going LOCO. Two incredibly even races, up to 100 mph! What a fluke!

Then - after leaning out his window - Frank sank back into the bucket seat...giddy with laughter - waving a five dollar bill in my face.

FRANK: "WOW, they gave up! The driver handed me the five, then drove away."

I was shocked! I had NOT actually won decisively. Why pay up?

Why would this GSX skedaddle after 2 exceedingly close races?

Ah...mystery solved: "Parental curfew!"

Yeah, that HAD to be it: This spoiled rich kid had to have Daddy's GSX "home by midnight."

Therefore...he must BE OBEDIENT or face the dreaded consequences: Grounded 2 weeks with no supper!

But now - after nearly getting whipped by BUICK'S new muscle car; I had to GET SERIOUS: Time marches on. 1969 was long gone: summer 1970 would no longer be another gravy-train of red light pushovers: 340 Dart Swingers. GSX Buicks. 454 LS Chevelles. 426 Hemi-cudas. LT-1 Camaros. Six-Pack Dodge Super Bees - W-30 442s - stalking the asphalt jungle of Market Street - like warriors seeking battle.

But no way was I about to surrender.

Chapter 31

A 1970 SS 454 Chevelle

JULY- 1970:

Understandably- after nearly getting stir-fried by a super-fast Buick GSX- I likened myself to a P-51 Mustang pilot - early 1945 - after his initial encounter with a Nazi ME 262 JET fighter: "WOW!...that Kraut almost BLEW ME away! DAMM...how FAST was he going?"

Indeed, the differences in speed of the 1970s muscle cars - vs. 1969 - was like moving forward into the "jet era" of street racing. Seemingly in a "flash," everything had changed.

Hence, the new, unwritten "street rules of engagement" mandated that either you "up gun" OR transfer to a "desk job" (i.e.) Stay home Friday nights - watching "Room 222"..." Brady Bunch"..."That Girl,"..."Love American Style," etc.

Could Mom's GTO - still a formidable street fighter- be nearing obsolescence?

In handgun parlance, Mom's goat was a snub-nosed, six-shot.38 revolver – pitted against 9 mm ten-shot automatics.

QUOTE:

"NEVER bring a knife to a gunfight."

Like Kenny Rogers sez..."Ya gotta know wenda hold 'em; and know wenda foldem."

Previously, I'd been pitching a "perfect" game. BUT now, was it time to head for the dugout? I felt like Lee at Appomattox, who wrote..."it seemed pointless to continue the battle."

It was only a matter of time before some voracious LS 454 Chevelle SS (450 horses) would show me his taillights - the absolute WORST feeling a street racer can experience. Youngstown had always been a "Chevy town." Hence, LS Chevelles were "flying off the shelves..."selling like hot cakes," etc.

On Market one night, alongside me was a red LS Chevelle 454. Looking over at the driver (mid 20s clean cut) I kept giving him animated hand signals..."wanna race...wanna race?"

Looking over, he became John McEnroe..."YOU CANNOT BE SERIOUS!" He pulled away gently from the light - greatly amused about the VERY idea of being challenged by "another pig" GTO.

Mom's GTO was indeed extremely fast. But consider the odds: Was it realistic to think that a 400 cubic inch Pontiac GTO could prevail over a 454 cubic inch LS Chevelle? Or a 426 Hemi-cuda?

It was like matching a welter weight 165 lb. champ vs a 225 lb. heavyweight contender.

Who brings the greater punching power? Driving on Market now had become a brand new ballgame, with me like a stiff old player - approaching retirement.

Sooner or later, some 440 six pack Superbee would blow me away. They were prowling everywhere.

Even Roadrunners now came with the much-feared A-12 tripower option.

"SIGH".... If ONLY I could go back to summer 1969 on Market street. It was like singing.

"Jingle Bells" in July: "Oh, what fun it is to ride in a GTO- 350 horses pulling away."

I was like a crap-shooter playing with "loaded" dice. Every night I would be "on a roll."

It was a different story at every red light, but always the ending would be the same: Some bad boy in some muscle car would line up against me, but after the light changed, I'd be waving "bye-bye."

But now - like an amateur performer on the trapeze- I was hanging on DESPERATELY for dear life: (play Eagles "Desperado")

By spring 1970, the sheet hit the fan: Now EVERY car company had jumped onto the fast car bandwagon. it was all so surreal: So hard to grasp.

Even American (Nash Rambler) Motors had a new MUSCLE CAR prowling about!

To me, this was like Schwinn introducing a MOTORCYCLE: WHERE DOES IT ALL END?

Chrysler had overwhelmed the market with a plethora of rocket-fast new models; and virtually all could be had with the so-called "giant killer" 340.

Market street - once my utopia - had become a horrible dystopian nightmare!

And then, to my even GREATER dismay, frumpy old FORD now introduced their ALL NEW line of street muscle: Cobra jet Mustang. Cobra jet Torino. Cobra jet Fairlane. Mercury Cyclone Cobra jet. Even a Mercury Cougar Cobra jet.

A 1970 Ford Torino Cobra Jet

This gave me a wild idea! Start an all new airline company; and call it (of course) COBRA JET AIRLINES! Think about it: Would a passenger buy a cross-country flight on United, or would they rather fly COBRA JET? Imagine a hot stewardess - wearing her Cobra jet logo cap - greeting all the disembarking passengers..."Have a good stay, sir...and thanks for flying Cobra Jet!"

Ah, the blessings of American free enterprise: Start one's own company - becoming filthy rich.

But there was no escaping reality: All U.S. car manufacturers were humming along - literally overwhelming the market with hot new cars - designed SPECIFICALLY to blow away hot shots at red lights.

For me, it was going from 1969's EUPHORIA to 1970's PARANOIA!

Now on Market street at night, I'd be keenly aware of all my surroundings; like a US army scout, assigned to the "point" in south Vietnam.

Even worse: I was now being LAUGHED at, by drivers behind the wheel of these newer, faster 1970s muscle cars.

At a light one night on Market, alongside pulls up a new AAR 1970 Barracuda with its fearsome tri power 340: a fat guy (double chin) was behind the wheel. After hand signaling him to race me, he shot back..."Hah hah! - unless you wanna race for five, I wouldn't waste my time."

Fatty didn't look very time-constrained to me. Nevertheless, I was forced to eat a slice of humble pie. I felt totally humiliated!

Then, it only got worse: SETTING: a Saturday afternoon, on the north side, at a red light on Fifth Ave. Alongside pulls up Keith Stone - driving a new, blue '70 Buick Gran Sport with "Stage One" engine callouts. I'd known "Stoney" as an old boy scout friend (7th-8th grade). Light changes...WHA-ROOM! Stoney's Buick came streaking out of the hole- staying a mere fender behind me...till the end. Waving, he drove off. And ME? NEARLY whipped again!

Now, preoccupied with the fear of losing, sometimes I would even FORGET to play the 8-track. Deep in thought behind the wheel, I kept thinking..."How can I make Mom's goat faster?

Then an idea...the Sir Isaac Newton (gravity) solution: Make it LIGHTER. But how? Toss out spare and jack? Floor mats? Owner's manual? Road maps? Air cleaner? WHAT?

Ah, the gas tank! Fill no more above 1/8...save a lot of weight. And so - while driving around - the needle would slosh between 1/4 and "E."

But this quickly became a total nuisance- stopping everyday - just to buy a puny allotment of premium gas? How insane was that? The people working at the Belmont Sunoco began to hate me with a passion! (can't blame 'em)

Then...the AWAKENING: I now came to realize that just to keep my victory string intact, I was at the threshold of insanity (i.e.) going NUTS...completely LOCO! I knew Mom's GTO was now badly outgunned on the street; but I just couldn't come to "grips" with it.

It was just like an aging, ex-superstar actress - who keeps waiting for that ONE last exciting movie script to come her way: but she knows it's only delusions of grandeur. Time has passed her by. Never again would her name appear at the top of the marquee.

Likewise, how much longer could my delusions of grandeur - about Mom's GTO remaining undefeated – go on? The clock was ticking. The sand - running through the hourglass. I just couldn't accept the fact that time had moved on - leaving me stranded in a fantasy world of the past.

Chapter 32

AUGUST - 1970:

It was a bright Saturday afternoon: I was driving out Market Street to the mall.

DESTINATION: "Musicland" - a dynamite place to buy 8 track tapes at "close out" prices.

BINGO! I found "Chicago Transit Authority" and "Sly and the Family Stone's Greatest Hits" - both SIXTY PERCENT OFF.

Make my day!

Driving back home, being daytime - meant NO street racing. Too much traffic. Most serious street racers knew to only come out at night, when streets were less-traveled.

The traffic light ahead had just turned red: I was thinking about calling Cutie pie: "Should I call her? - or should I not?"

"To be, or not to be."I became Hamlet! - roiled by indecision.

Meanwhile, I hardly noticed the blue 1970 FORD Torino - stopping in the left lane beside me.

To me, no Ford was worth ANY attention; because, in my estimation, "Ford" was a "4 letter" word (crap).

Not since the 1965 Mustang GT 289 'hi-po,' did I regard Ford as being a serious player in the muscle car category.

I never respected ANY Ford. They were stodgy. Unappealing. Boring. A perfect car for a parish priest.

Throughout the 60s, Ford was never much of a player in America's street racing culture - preferring instead to design cars with "family appeal."

A top Ford seller was their "Country Squire" 9-passenger station wagon. Ugh. A down-sized municipal bus - disguised as an automobile. It would hog-up more than HALF your driveway.

Then I remembered fall 1965: the introduction of Ford's highly-touted 390 Fairlane GT - appearing with great fanfare on the front cover of "Car and Driver."

What a joke!

Ford's new 390 GT Fairlane was a "plain vanilla" car. At best, it could be judged as "looking okay." Rather humdrum for a so-called "muscle car." Not surprisingly, cheapskate STUPID Ford - instead of re-tooling for an all-new modernized engine - went instead with their old, TRADITIONAL 390 cubic inch V8: an engine with a TRADITION of practically LOSING every race. Ergo; I considered Ford's all-new 390 Fairlane GT to be a "flabby" muscle car – a pushover! A sled on 4 wheels.

A '66 Ford Fairlane GT

FLASHBACK: it was early summer 1965 at the Red Barn...a Saturday night: Cruising through the parking lot was Bruce Holtzman (who lived up my street) - acting like he's some total bad-azz - driving a brand new, 2-door, silver '65 Ford Galaxie; with "390" fender badges.

Then Georgie Simon pulls in - driving his mom's new, red 65 Mustang convertible - with "260 V8" fender badges; with a 3-speed console shifter; with the top down.

Nice car! Simon's "foxy" Mustang was surrounded immediately. Since Georgie and Bruce lived across the street from one another, predictably, calls went out for the two neighbors to RACE one another.

Everyone followed the two out Belmont; to the Rt 304 red light.

Light changes to green! And you guessed it: Immediately, underdog Georgie - shifting the 3-speed 'stang- forges out to a 2 car lead; then wins GOING AWAY.

Bruce Holtzman never again would he be seen at Red Barn - thoroughly ashamed because his "MIGHTY" 390 had been dusted by a little, 260 cube "mini V8." Par for the course: 390 Fords were universal DOGS- feared by NO ONE!

Flashback: Fall 1965:

There was a new kid in school: Chuck Mulholland; a die-hard Ford man; whose father owned a machine shop. Chuck sat behind Frankie Malone, in junior English class.

Beginning of October, daddy bought Chuckie a white, automatic 1966 Fairlane GT - red interior; with a 4-barrel 390 V8 under thehood.

Chuckie was on cloud nine - driving his new dream car!

During second period lunch, "proud Chuckie" would sit down at our table with Frank and me; then he'd play "make believe."

Chuck - with a straight face - would try to make us BELIEVE his doggy 390 Fairlane had dusted a litany of really fast cars.

Said Chuckie: "I beat 383 Dodge"..."I beat a 283 Malibu"..."I beat a 289 Mustang." "I beat a 389 Grand Prix." "I beat a 327 Chevy."

Whoa there, Chuckie-boy!

A 390 Ford defeating a 327 Chevy? That was likely as a blizzard sweeping through Death Valley- in July. Of course, it was all bluster!

Finally, Billy Stankovich, had heard quite enough- challenging Chuck to race his 4-barrel 65 GTO - a burgundy hard top. Console Hurst 4-speed shifter.

It was all set: the two would meet Friday midnight at the Mahoning Ave Burger Chef. It was no contest at all! Word was that Stankovich's GTO had destroyed Chucky's Fairlane by SIX car lengths! A totally humiliating beat down! As the saying goes: "Never bring a knife to a gunfight." Needless to say, Chuck Mulholland never again drove his Fairlane GT to school - wisely choosing to ride the school bus It certainly spelled the end of all his DELUSIONAL bragging.

Suddenly, back to reality: The blue Torino in the left lane displayed "DRAG PACK" fender badges - plainly in my view: I'd been caught "daydreaming."

I'd read all about "drag pack" Torino FORDS...designed ESPECIALLY for street racing: Massive 429 cubic inch Cobra Jet engine - standard: A huge 780 cfm Holley 4 barrel carb. Close ratio 4-speed. 390 gears.

High capacity oil pump. Special Detroit Locker differential. Forged aluminum pistons. Special cast-iron manifold. 11.3-to-one compression ratio. High-lift, long-duration, solid lifter camshaft.

A real, down 'n dirty street-fightin' machine! Probably cranking out close to 500 hp!

I thought..."Relax man...It's STILL a Ford."Light changes to green! It was like I'd brought a switchblade to an artillery duel.

The Torino effortlessly and TOTALLY blew Mom's goat into oblivion! I thought it was a bad dream.

By the time the Torino began to slow down, he was FIVE car lengths ahead. It was a terrible moment in my life. I STILL remember it. I refused to believe my eyes!

Of course I knew one day I would LOSE...but by five cars? I always figured it would be a 6-pack 440 Roadrunner: Or a monster 454 LS Chevelle; or maybe a 426 Hemi-cuda.

Now in total shock, I asked (axed) the Torino driver to "pop his hood."

Holy macaroni! His engine looked big enough to power "Mayberry RFD." It was a huge MONSTER. The unmistakable, "new car smell" was apparent.

"Well, nice race man. Good luck. You got a really fast car."

The Torino drove away - leaving me totally mortified - thinking..."THIS CAN'T BE HAPPENING!

"Losing by FIVE CARS! FIVE car lengths!"

To me, it was like Usain Bolt - losing by FIVE yards in the hundred meters. Totally unfathomable!

I was parked at curbside on Market street - profoundly shook to the depths of my soul.

I now realized a milestone had been crossed; with no point of return: Mom's GTO was NO longer undefeated (i.e.) "the party" was OVER.

Ergo, I had no alternative; other than "denying reality." Hence, I began a trip down memory lane...thinking of better times in the past. It was like one of those old Turner classic movies; where the film begins in "flash-back" mode:

I recalled:

- My first race in Mom's GTO; and how badly I'd destroyed a 4-speed SS 396 Chevelle...by SIX car lengths.

- The astonished reaction by the greasers at Clark gas station - after beating Gary Conner's 427 Chevelle; the fastest car around.

- Beating a 66 tripower GTO- supposedly, the fastest goat on the north side

- I recalled my underdog, astonishing, defeat of "Hercules," driving his 66 427 Vette convertible.

A 66 427 Corvette Convertible

- I remembered that wild Friday night on Market street - blowing away four different '69 Roadrunners- during a 3 hour marathon of racing!

- My blow-out race out Belmont Ave extension; with a 69 440 Charger RT.

- Another wild, 140 MPH high-speed freeway race, with a 440 GTX Plymouth.

- Finally, my most unlikely, implausible victory: a 426 Hemi roadrunner.

Undoubtedly, this was the most exciting, thrilling, satisfying, gratifying triumph of my life - even to today. This may sound uncanny, but to me, defeating a mighty street Hemi was like winning a personalized Congressional Medal of Honor. I was a hero to myself - displaying great courage in the face of overwhelming odds (i.e.) 426 cubes. Dual 4-barrel carbs. 425 horses.

Never can I forget those bright headlights five feet beside me - the hemi straining mightily to "pull even." How its front end angled high above the pavement- under max acceleration. The ear-shattering noise of those two 4 barrel carbs - thundering like a volcano. How could I ever forget? A for sure underdog- winning a most unlikely victory. It was like David beating Goliath. Sampson slaying the entire Philistine army. The 300 Spartans at Thermopylae. The outnumbered 20th Maine at "Little Round Top" - intrepidly fending off a full-blown charge, by determined Confederate veterans, at Gettysburg.

Then I recalled all my most memorable events - from child to adult.

- At four: when Dad took the training wheels off my Huffy bicycle - riding on TWO wheels for the first time! I felt liberated. I now could ride around the block!

- At five; when AT LAST, I could tie my own shoes...no need to ever call Mom again.

- At seven - first time riding "no hands" on my bike- going down Bradley Lane. Look Mom...no hands!

- At 14 - awarded the coveted Eagle Scout rank...29 merit badges.

- At 16, watching the Ohio drivers' license examiner- signing off that I'd PASSED! Liberated again!

- AT 17, on a summer day in June; driving my cousin Mona's amazingly fast, new 65 GTO...a day I'd NEVER forget.

- At 18, opening that letter from Ohio State - announcing I'd been awarded an academic scholarship. I was no longer beholden to attending tiny "Youngstown College."

- On my first "date" at Ohio State, behind Morrill Tower... my first French kiss.

Despite all these unforgettable, once-in-a-lifetime events-all would pale in comparison: Beating that Roadrunner 426 Hemi: my ultimate life experience.

Even better: that I was a decided UNDERDOG, made it even more memorable.

In fact, in almost every race, I was the underdog - who always won. But no longer. It was all so incredibly IRONIC: I was deeply in thought - trying to put it all into perspective.

Suddenly; everything came into focus: A remarkable similarity of sorts. I recalled that enduring scene from "Godfather" - after the meeting of the "Dons" - from New York's "five families."

"All along... it was Barzini; but I didn't know, until this day."

- Don Corleone

(and for me)

"All along, it would be a FORD; but I wouldn't know it...until today."

THE END

My Mother's GTO

Rick Sandine